ESSENTIAL
ENERGY
BALANCING

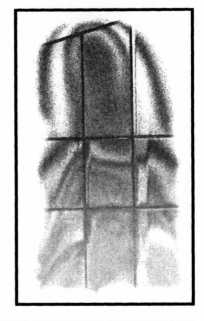

The beautiful rainbow Lady on the cover of this book is an appearance of Brede, who is my Goddess and the source of the Lords of Karma and Essential Energy Balancing® systems. The image "just appeared" on the glass side of a finance company office building in Clearwater, Florida in 1994. Science has not been able to explain the sixty-foot, two-story image, and most people assume it to be of Mary. The site quickly became a shrine for people of all faiths until a Christian group bought the building in 1998. Brede no longer works her healing magick through the glass, but the colors and the image remain. The photograph was taken by Thomas Swann on Winter Solstice 1996.

Other books by Diane Stein

A Woman's I Ching

All Women Are Healers

All Women Are Psychics

Casting the Circle

Essential Reiki

Essential Reiki Workshop

Healing with Flower and Gemstone Essences

Healing with Gemstones & Crystals

The Holistic Puppy

The Lords of Karma and Energy Balancing
A Workshop with Diane Stein

Natural Healing for Dogs & Cats

Natural Remedy Book for Dogs & Cats

Natural Remedy Book for Women

Prophetic Visions of the Future

Psychic Healing with Spirit Guides and Angels

We are the Angels

ESSENTIAL ENERGY BALANCING

An Ascension Process

DIANE STEIN

CROSSING PRESS
Berkeley

For Sue and for Brede

Crossing Press and the Crossing Press colophon are registered trademarks
of Random House, Inc.

Library of Congress Cataloging-in-Publication Data
Stein, Diane, 1948–
        Essential energy balancing / by Diane Stein.
            p. cm.
        Includes bibliographical references and index.
        1. Karma—Miscellanea. 2. Force and energy—Miscellanea. I. Title.
    BF1045.K37 S735   2000
    131—dc21   99-057492

ISBN 9781580910286

Printed in the United States of America

Cover design by Victoria May
Cover photograph by Thomas Swann

15 14 13 12 11 10 9 8 7 6 5

First Edition

Acknowledgments

I would like to thank several women who have been instrumental in the development of Essential Energy Balancing®. Karen Silverman has been involved in these explorations from the beginning, and has offered suggestions and tried each process along the way. Her son Josh, at five years old, discovered the I AM Template and taught me about children and the Lords of Karma. Corinne Nichols offered valuable suggestions, especially in the later Lords of Karma processes and in Essential Energy Balancing® Processes VII and VIII. Copper and Kali, my Siberian husky dogs, discovered their Energy Selves and have entered ascension with me. Copper says he's done it a few times before. He probably has.

Francena Hancock has followed me in bringing in a Goddess and has helped me to understand what is the process and what is "only me." Ginger Grancagnolo has shared her impressions, feedback, and personal experiences. I also thank the patient women of the earliest Essential Energy Balancing® weekends who put up with my hesitations and incomplete understanding, and with my irritability from holding the system's (and Brede's) high energy.

And always, of course, I thank Brede—discarnate author of the process and of all the healing in my life.

Contents

Diagrams

Introduction

As those people I have taught Essential Energy Balancing® to know, I have had a hard time describing it in words. It can only be experienced. I was given the system step by step, channeled for and through me by my Goddess Brede, with instructions rather than explanations. I had been working with the Lords of Karma for two years and had suffered my first episodes of severe energy damage when Brede gave me the initial Energy Balancing process. I followed her directions for a request to the Lords of Karma, and she dictated the next and then the next requests. At the end of the meditation sequence I felt the first relief and hope for self-healing in a very long time.

My energy damage began on September 3, 1996. I was in a deep meditative state and during it, in great joy, fell asleep. But an hour or so later I awoke in agony. My contact with Brede and the Lords of Karma was gone, and my psychic senses and ability to leave my body were totally shut down. Physically, I felt numb and burning hot. Emotionally, I was devastated. I felt that my mind didn't work, and neither did my healing abilities. This extreme distress continued for several months, leaving me cut off completely from my guides and companions for so many years. Of all the in-body healers I trusted to help me, for six months no one was willing to place their hands on me or try. I cried for three months straight. One morning, Brede came in audibly for the first time since the damage and said, "Ask the Lords of Karma to align all of your energy bodies." Thus began Process I of Essential Energy Balancing® and the beginning of my healing and repair.

I later learned that the energy damage had been equivalent to a physical electrocution and was caused by off-planet negative interference. My Astral Twin/Inner Child died in the energy attack and it took six months to regenerate her sufficiently so that further healing could begin. Brede, the Lords of Karma, and my discarnate healers were working for me all the time, but I had no awareness of them. No healers in body would touch me because until the Astral Twin had regrown, there was nothing they could do—they knew this intuitively, although I did not. If I disbelieved in negative interference (as so many people do), I had learned the hard way. Another major energy attack occurred on August 13, 1997 and two lesser ones later that year and there have been more. Brede and the Lords of Karma developed Essential Energy Balancing® to save my life.

I had no idea then that the technique would contain ten processes besides the methods for working with the Lords of Karma, and would become a complete and independent system of healing for others. I understood that the processes were designed to heal core soul energy damage, but had no idea how total and complex the healing would be or how far reaching. Nor did I know, until I received the final process, that Brede's healing meditations are a process of ascension. Because of the energy damage, this process was triggered for me only after a year and a half of self-healing work (May 1, 1998 on Beltane). For most other people, however, the meditation sequence and the teaching about the Lords of Karma can be given in a weekend intensive or by reading this book. A four-CD set of the complete Essential Energy Balancing® and a videotape on the Lords of Karma basic process are both available from The Crossing Press.

Once the full process is experienced, Essential Energy Balancing® triggers a six-month or longer sequence of clearing, healing, and energy repatterning on all levels—physical/etheric, emotional, mental, spiritual, Core Soul, and DNA. These changes result in the healing and release of one-half to three-quarters (or more) of all the karma brought into this incarnation lifetime. All Core Soul damage is cleared and healed; the DNA is repaired and reconnected to twelve strands and ultimately to twenty-one strands for most people. Also, there is a reconnection and merging with your Higher Self, Essence Self, Goddess Self/Oversoul, and reconnection with Goddess.

The energy evolution and raising of vibration triggered by these important healings is called ascension in the metaphysical West and enlightenment in Eastern traditions. It has previously required many years of esoteric study and meditation to accomplish, and only a few adepts have ever accomplished it. Now it may be done in a few days of meditation work, then followed by six months of deep inner change. Most people will wish to do the process more slowly—this is highly positive, as well. Change is never easy and the clearing can be difficult, but it is well worth doing the work. You will be permanently rejoined with your Goddess-Within, and released from all karmic debt and all requirement to reincarnate on Earth (though some will choose to do so). The effect of this in daily life is permanent bliss and joy.

Brede is my own Goddess. She began to join with me before I became aware of her presence in June 1983, when I experienced a walk-in. A portion of who I was at that time was lifted from me and taken away, and a new spirit self (a part of Brede's spirit self) entered. I remember the walk-in incident clearly, though it occurred while I was in a lucid dream state and I did not understand what it meant for several more years. From that moment my life became a psychic, spiritual, and Goddess-based quest in every way. It had not been so before.

I first met Brede consciously in September 1991, though she had been channeling my writing and teaching all along. On a workshop trip, a woman brought me two framed photos of an incredibly lovely woman. The photos could not have been of any woman in an Earth body, and photographers I show them to still argue about how the images happened on the film. The Lady wears a crown of roses in her hair and sunflowers in a belt at her waist, and her body glows with radiant golden light. Her hair is reddish gold, her eyes are closed or looking down (they are bright blue), and her face is so peaceful and beautiful that I started to cry when I looked at it. "Who is she?" I had to ask.

The pictures had appeared on a roll of film taken at Medjuggore, in what was then Yugoslavia, now Bosnia. The photographer saw no image until the film was developed and had almost thrown the film away. Since 1982, sightings of supposedly Mary have occurred at Medjuggore and the small town has become a world shrine to Her. That night meditating with the pictures, however, when the woman came in to talk with me, I asked her, "Are you Mary?" She replied, "No." "Are you Persephone then?" I asked, Persephone being the first spring flower Goddess to come to mind. "No," she said, "but that's close." I asked how she was to be called and she said, "You may call me The Maiden for now."

She said that she had not had a priestess in a thousand years and asked if I would be her priestess. I unhesitatingly agreed. I asked if she was a healer like me, and if she would like to work through my hands. She replied that I could ask for her presence when I did healing and she would come, but would participate only "when she was needed." After that night I began asking her to come in whenever I did healing or ritual work, and I always felt her presence or heard her voice. She also often talks to me while I am meditating.

During a healing about a month later, The Maiden informed me that her name was Brede. We know her in the United States as Bridget or Brigit, but she prefers the Celtic pronunciation, so I spell it phonetically. Other spellings of her name are Brigid, Bridgh, or Bride, and in Eastern Europe the pronunciation is more like "Breet." In Scandinavia she is called Freya. She was the Great Goddess of Eastern and Western Europe for more than a thousand years, and when Christianity could not erase her, she became St. Bridgit.

Brede has worked through me consciously for my writing, teaching, and healing since that time. A number of other photographs of her have been given to me over the years. One was taken in Denver, when a dying child asked her mother to "take a picture of the pretty lady" whom the mother couldn't see. Several others were taken at Medjuggore, and like the first photos, appeared on the film when it was exposed, though the photographer saw nothing when taking the picture. Brede's picture is on the cover of my book *Psychic Healing with Spirit Guides and Angels* (The Crossing Press, 1996). She has appeared in a number of sightings in various countries, and though she is thought to be Mary, Mary is not appearing on Earth at this time.

Brede's latest manifestation on Earth is a rainbow image on the glass window of an office building in Clearwater, Florida (at the corner of Drew St. and I-19). It is pictured on the cover of this book. Brede has joined with me fully in my own ascension process and is the source creator of Essential Energy Balancing® as she has given it through me. She has blessed me and my life in every way and will likewise bless yours through this process. She is always and always will be pure love.

The other Gods and Goddesses to thank for Essential Energy Balancing® are the Lords of Karma, known also as the Karmic Council or Karmic Board, or the Angels or Spirits of Karma, the Recording Angels, or the Lipika. They have been known through all religions and all times. These highest-level Ascended Masters (male and female) have granted people on Earth the greatest possible blessing—a method for healing us by releasing and freeing us of karma. This is a rapid, easy method, almost as easy as asking for it. Most suffering can now be healed, for the first time in Earth herstory.

We have been granted this karmic grace because it is time for both Earth and Earth's people to evolve beyond cause and effect, eye-for-an-eye relating. The weight of human action and pain is holding back the growth of the planet. Each living Be-ing (human and otherwise) *is* the planet. It is time for Earth to increase her evolution, to raise her vibrational light to new and higher levels, to ascend to higher dimensions. This can only be done by achieving people's raised, ascended, and evolved vibrational levels through karmic healing.

We have for the first time been given very easy methods for healing karma and personal suffering, because the planet will not otherwise survive. The raising of Earth's (and Earth people's) energy and awareness is crucial to raise and heal the energy of the planet. Remember that the Earth is a living Goddess and we are her collective consciousness. Earth's ascension is her means of survival, of healing the damage done to her through overpopulation, pollution, violence, and desecration. Only by healing Earth's people and raising their vibrational levels to ascension can the planet be healed. This must happen rapidly because the damage is great and time is running out. The process must be simple because a critical mass of people must be reached to tip the balance. The time is now, and we are the healers and healed of planet Earth who must accomplish it.

The Lords of Karma are multiple groups of enlightened discarnate Be-ings. A karmic group of nine to eleven Ascended Masters works with each soul group of people in bodies on Earth. They decide with each individual before birth/incarnation what lessons are to be learned in the coming lifetime. Each lifetime is a part of the overall plan of numerous lifetimes and a course of learning for the purpose of soul development, evolution, and growth. With the individual's full agreement, the Lords of Karma are the directors of the incarnation's primary events and conditions. Upon birth into the Earth body we forget both who we are and who they are, and we lose all contact with them.

Using the processes of this book, the Lords of Karma may be directly accessed and requested to complete the lessons immediately. In most cases they will agree to the requests, and personal karma then becomes cooperative and co-creative. This is the equivalent of receiving a diploma (and all its learning) without ever going to school, a sort of karmic Ph.D. Since we have done these lessons again and again through many previous lifetimes, the release from further repetition is welcome and much needed. It is also a shortcut to the vibrational ascension of people and of Earth.

The many soul groups of the Lords of Karma are headed by an intergalactic supervisory board. We are not the only sentient Be-ings or inhabited planet or dimension—there are many. Comprised of both women and men, the supervisory members are the Ascended Masters most people are familiar with, if they know of the Masters at all. Some of their names are El Morya, St. Germaine, Athena, Kwan Yin, Ashtar, Isis, Mary, Cyclopea, Balthor, Kuthumi, and Sananda. The Ascended

Masters come from a variety of planets, races, and cultures. One or more of them may make themselves known to you as your vibration clears and is raised through healing and releasing your personal karma. One Be-ing in particular to know about is Lady Nada, who is the Keeper of the Karma of the Earth. Some of us know her as The Great Mother or Great Goddess. Brede, The Maiden, is Keeper of the Earth Grid, and is sometimes known as Little Nada.

The first visual impression I had of Nada occurred while working with my Lords of Karma group. I asked for a release that was under debate ("Should we grant this?") and Nada was consulted. She has the final say to all requests and she granted mine. She appeared to me as a tall, almost gaunt woman of at least middle age who was obviously pregnant. To some people she appears in younger form. I asked her, "Why do you still have to go through childbirth at your age? It's not fair." She replied, "All things are born through me." Her name in Spanish means "nothing." She is the Buddhist Void or pregnant dark womb from which all creation manifests. Nothing exists without her or without passing through her darkness. She is particularly powerful at releasing and healing karmic attachments and patterns, and negative interference. Your Lords of Karma group will request her presence as needed for your healing, and she will appear when any request has planetary consequences.

Karma is who we are on Earth, but it does not exist on most other inhabited planets. Karma only exists through the fifth dimension. Earth has been a third-dimensional planet and has very recently been raised to the fourth dimension overall, and karma is on its way out. By giving us conscious access to the Lords of Karma and to a simple method of karmic release, we are being propelled toward that fifth-dimensional reality where karma no longer exists as the primary means of soul growth and human evolutionary learning. Achieving a critical mass of people who are consciously healing their karma is the key to ending karma on Earth. As they raise their vibrational status and ascend to the fifth dimension, the planet herself is also raised.

Karma is usually defined as action and reaction, or cause and effect. It can also be known positively as choice and change, or more negatively as an eye for an eye. The idea of an action having a direct and exact opposite reaction is usually believed, but is not true. If you have been raped in this lifetime it does not mean you were a rapist in your last incarnation. To believe so is simplistic and usually incorrect. It is also destructive for an individual's soul growth and real understanding.

Rather, think of karma as energy and vibration, just as human (and all life's) existence is energy and vibration. The energy of one's thoughts and acts becomes who you are. A negative action, like a murder, remains in your energy (in your Mind Grid specifically) as part of you until it is released. This release can happen in a number of ways, and being murdered by someone else is possible but not the most likely. More important than receiving a like action in return is the learning that the action was wrong. The only release is through understanding on every level that murder is wrong, and the only true resolution is never to commit it again. Negative actions and lifetimes are a part of the development of every soul—to learn about something in the Earth body we must experience it. Everyone has done negative things. Most people will not do them again because they have learned a better way from the experience.

The major part of karma, however, is not wrongs committed that remain in one's energy but wrongs received. The woman who is raped, for example, holds the damage in her energy at all levels—physical, emotional, mental, and spiritual. If that damage is not healed in the lifetime when the rape occurred, it carries over to future incarnations. In some way and at some time the damage must be released from the woman's energy. In a future lifetime she may meet her rapist again, either as another perpetrator or as someone who will affect her healing. Or there may be someone different as her perpetrator, or a different yet similar situation. If she experiences rape again it is for the purpose of "opening the wound" for another opportunity for full healing and release of the rape energy. In this way, the issue is resolved so she can receive the healing. If she is raped again, the rape becomes Core Soul damage and its energy carries on through lifetime after lifetime until the healing occurs.

Most karma, then, is suffering from past lives that has not been healed and the subsequent energy remains a part of one's soul vibration. This is why karmic patterns develop, where a woman who has been raped finds that she has had a variety of past lives where she was also raped or otherwise sexually abused. Feminists today talk about "breaking the chain" of the abuse of women and children. This is done by healing the damage so the energy of pain is removed from a person's vibrational makeup. Therapists try to do this, but their work is usually too close to the physical body to heal the damage in the Core Soul. Where formerly the chain of events had to be replayed and replayed until healing occurred, now the damage may be released by asking the Lords of Karma to heal it through all the energy levels and lifetimes.

When this request is granted, the pattern is broken, the damage is repaired on all levels, and the energy of that particular suffering is removed totally. The woman will not be raped again and will heal the damage that rape in this and other lifetimes has created. Each time a piece of karmic suffering is healed, more light can enter and the woman's overall vibration is raised. With the release of many sufferings from her soul and psyche, all the karmic patterns of pain may be completed and ended. The woman who was raped has had other sufferings in her life, as we all have. By requesting and receiving releases from the Lords of Karma for all the suffering she is aware of, more and more light and healing will pour into her Be-ing. The implications of this gift of clearing and release are immense—transformational life changes for everyone.

As the individual's karma clears, so does the planet's. Karma is held in personal energy in the Mind Grid, the Core Soul upper octave of the mental body. The Mind Grid appears in psychic vision as a domed golden screen or mesh. As each piece of karma is cleared, a knot or tear is healed in the Grid, and a series of thought forms about what reality consists of is released. Each individual's Mind Grid is connected and intermeshed with a larger grid, that of the Earth's. The Earth Grid is the planet's collective consciousness. As each piece of karma is removed from one's personal Mind Grid, it is also removed from the Earth Grid. When everyone has healed her karma and the karmic damage of having been raped, rape will no longer exist as part of the consciousness of the planet, and no one will suffer rape again. While the healing of every single woman who has been raped is not necessary to achieve this, a critical mass of numbers is required. There is finally a way out of all the damage and suffering.

When an individual has healed more than half of the suffering and soul damage (karma) she has brought into and experienced in this lifetime, she may be granted ascension. Ascension means release from the wheel of karma, the necessity for continuous rebirths and repeated suffering on Earth. It also means raising one's vibrational energy to fifth-dimensional levels or higher. Many people, certainly most healers, have incarnated on Earth countless times, even thousands of times. We have experienced the planet in all of her pain and lived the third-dimensional reality with her. Now we may evolve and leave the pain behind. If we do reincarnate on Earth again, it will only be by choice.

The current Earth changes demand the cleaning up of human violence, destruction, and lack of love both for ourselves and the planet as a whole. These negatives do not and cannot exist at higher vibrational levels and the Earth cannot ascend to higher levels with them. They are equivalent to the woman's soul damage from unhealed rape. When enough of the violence, destruction, and lack of love are healed in people on Earth, the planet may also enter ascension. Karma will then no longer exist on Earth for any of Earth's people, because the need for repeated lessons will no longer exist. Violence, destruction, and lack of love will be removed from the Earth Grid and from all people. The planet and all its life forms will then move to the fifth vibrational dimension and beyond.

The processes in this book offer ways to heal your personal suffering and release the karma and karmic patterns that continue it. For those who are in their last lifetime on Earth, it is necessary to heal what remains of Earth karma before we are free to leave here. Earth is combat duty for those healers who are the interplanetary troubleshooters of the universe. A large number of healers are incarnated at this time for the purpose of raising the vibration of people and the Earth to the point where ascension (personal and planetary) is accomplished. In the East these people are called bodhisattvas. They have healed their own karma and are no longer required to return, but do so to heal others and the planet. Many bodhisattvas are incarnated on Earth now, though only some know consciously who they are.

Animals, by the way, also have karma, past lives, Core Souls, Energy Selves, and participate in Goddess. They have as complex an energy structure as our own and it is similar to ours. The pets we share our lives with may be fragments of our own Goddess Self/Oversouls. The complexities of karma and reincarnation are the same for animals as for humans, and the methods of karmic release and Essential Energy Balancing® apply to them. They are also being prepared for ascension at this time, and may find it easier to accomplish than people. Pets' karma is usually tied to the people they live with, and they may have lived with the same people many times in many incarnations. Dogs, cats, and horses can reincarnate interchangeably—an animal who is a dog now may have been a horse the last time around. People who clear their karma will find that they can help their pets to clear theirs. When people enter ascension, their animal familiars usually do it with them, if the pet hasn't achieved it already.

Entering ascension means a great change in the structure and Light of one's personal energy. First, our two-strand DNA is returned to the twelve strands we settled on Earth with, and eventually in the ascension process it may be increased to twenty-one strands or more. With the release of karmic pain and the clearing of the Mind Grid, much more Light (defined as energy, information, input of Goddess) may enter one's energy system, resulting in the healing of all energy damage. This healing occurs on levels never before reached with other methods of healing, levels never before attainable while incarnated. The energy bodies and chakras undergo great change with new chakras, chakra systems, energy bodies, and other components developed, activated, and opened.

Ascension also means rejoining with your Goddess Self, your Oversoul Goddess Within. (For a few women only it means complete joining of your life energy with your Goddess, a higher level.) Having the Goddess in your life on a daily basis makes for a much different life from what you now experience. Your psychic abilities increase as does your ability to create a bountiful and joyful life of service to others and the Earth. We have been separated from Source for so long, we have been totally isolated from our spirits and from who we really are. This ends now, and the sense of coming home is tremendously gratifying. Your Goddess Self (or Goddess) also represents total unconditional love. Once the ascension process is completed you will never be without that total love again; the love is always there within you. You will never be lonely again. You will also finally understand—for the first time in Earth incarnation—who you really are as spirit in a body, as a Be-ing of love and Light. The forgetting that was necessary at birth is no longer required and much of the memory returns.

It is important to note that karma can be healed only while in a body. While we have access to much greater energy levels, knowledge, awareness, and consciousness between lifetimes, karma accrued while in body must be healed in body. The body must be respected and cared for, and the incarnation respected, as the only means of healing karmic damage. Karmic release and the energy changes and evolution that result in ascension can happen only while one is in a body, too. Our complete healing and the healing of the Earth can be affected only by people on Earth. Though the Ascended Masters and Lords of Karma are waiting, desperately eager to help us, they can't do it for us. We are the ones in bodies and the Earth is our planet. The healing of karma and attainment of ascension is attained by everyday people—with the help of divine intervention and grace.

What this means is that while this book or an Essential Energy Balancing® workshop or set of tapes can teach you the techniques, your karmic healing and process of ascension lie in your hands. To attain them you must choose to do the work and be willing to accept the changes in your energy and life. You must be willing to undergo the six months of transformation that is a death and rebirth initiation process. It can be difficult. You must take the work and your co-creation with the Lords of Karma and your higher Energy Selves seriously, with great respect. Above all, you must have the self-respect and self-love to know that you deserve this healing and deserve to be a Be-ing of Light and of Goddess (or God or whatever your own term is for Source).

Everything in these processes at every step of the way is subject to free will. This is the first law of the universe and it will never be violated by the Lords of Karma, the Goddess, or your Energy Selves. If at any point in the Essential Energy Balancing® or Lords of Karma process you choose to stop, that wish will be honored, though it is a shame to stop the process before its completion. During the times when the healing and clearing become difficult and intense, it is tempting to call a halt. Especially at these times, gathering the courage to continue is important for your highest and best good.

It may also be difficult to face your greatest healing issues— the childhood incest, the things you did that were ethically wrong, the patterns you have avoided changing, the bad or destructive habits, and the negative relationships and relationship patterns—but this is your opportunity to clear and heal them forever. It may be difficult to know and briefly re-experience the sufferings of past lives. You will find that the pain of this life and the patterns of past ones are almost always intrinsically connected. However difficult it may be, facing and releasing these now is far easier than coming back for another incarnation to suffer the same patterns again. The easiest way out is to go forward and through.

The methods of this book and the Essential Energy Balancing® system were begun earlier in *We Are the Angels* (The Crossing Press, 1997). They are also available on a video from The Crossing Press. In that book and video, the basic Lords of Karma process and the first Energy Balancing meditation (divided into three parts) are presented. Since that time the system has developed and grown considerably. There are now four processes for working with the Lords of Karma to achieve karmic release and healing. They reach levels of healing the Core Soul that the basic process could not achieve. Essential Energy Balancing®, which depends on your ability to work with the Lords of Karma, now contains a sequence of ten meditative processes. I hesitate to call them meditations, as they are more correctly defined as Core Soul reprogrammings. These have become a unified system of energy and soul healing and a trigger into ascension.

Everything in these processes depends upon your ability to work with the Lords of Karma to heal and release your personal pain. Everyone's life is different and everyone has her own individual sufferings and healing issues. No one can do this healing for you, you must do it yourself with divine help. By learning to work co-creatively with the Lords of Karma for your own healing, the Essential Energy Balancing® system becomes individualized—it gives you what you need that may be different from what is useful to someone else.

However, the Essential Energy Balancing® meditative processes are the same for everyone and must be used the same way. Yet, each individual using them will go through her own specifically tailored healing of Core Soul damage and her own form of ascension. Everyone is unique and responds uniquely, with unique needs. Each person will receive what she needs, though the reprogramming sequences are the same for all.

The detailed information and diagrams on Core Soul structure are new to this book as well. The charts were given to me over a period of a year and a half by Brede. I often had no idea what she was showing me, but filled the information in on body outlines (created for me by Karen Narita, The Crossing Press art director). In my morning meditations, Brede would show me similar outlines, lit up with tiny points like Christmas lights to indicate the chakras or energy flows she wanted me to see. As time went on and the Essential Energy Balancing® system developed, the meaning of these charts became clearer. Yet, in the completion of ascension everything changed again.

The basic message is that we are very complicated Be-ings indeed. Since the charts and information are so complex, and since they are not directly necessary for going through the process, I have placed the energy structure information at the back of the book. I was afraid that using them sooner would frighten people off from the system or from picking up this book. If they are too complex for you at this time, skip them. Later they will make more sense. Once you understand them they become fascinating: we are more than we seem or than we will ever know.

Working with the Lords of Karma is for everyone who wants to do the work, while Essential Energy Balancing® is for more advanced healers. By working deeply with the Lords of Karma, however, you become ready to go forward. You are about to begin the adventure of your spiritual lifetime. I wish you well and Brede wishes you well on your journey to greater Light and joy.

THE
LORDS
OF
KARMA

Healing with the Lords of Karma

Anyone who chooses can learn to work with the Lords of Karma. I have taught this process in numerous adult workshops, and even to children. Occasionally it takes a few tries, and a few people may reach the Lords of Karma best by using a pendulum, but virtually everyone meets her karmic group easily and learns to work with them. Everybody's life is profoundly changed by the process, made easier and better by the gifts of karmic dispensation and the consequent release from suffering. This willingness on the Ascended Masters' part to hear us and heal us was not always available. Until quite recently, there was no option for release at all.

My first encounter with the Lords of Karma came during a healing I received about eight years ago. At that time I asked the healer for help with a situation that was major in my life, and that had not resolved in any other way. She asked me if I knew what my karmic contract for the issue was and when I didn't know she suggested I go to the Lords of Karma to find out. I had never heard the name and the idea of "lords" put me off, but I agreed to try it. When I asked to speak with the Lords of Karma, a line of people in black robes appeared in my psychic sight. They did not seem pleased to be called upon, and as I could not see their faces I assumed them all to be male. I asked my question and was given the answer in a few terse words.

The healer then suggested that I could ask to rewrite the contract, but if I did so, it might have serious consequences. "We were born into a pretty nice culture, with hot showers and flush toilets. That can change next time; don't make them mad," she said. She warned me to be very clear and careful about the wording of my request and what I wanted revised. "There are booby traps here," she told me. Working with the healer, and psychically with the other person involved, I devised my request and asked. I heard a one word response, "Granted," and the Lords of Karma were gone. The energy work that happened for me over the next several weeks at night, the colors and rainbows and feelings of joy and bliss, told me that something had indeed occurred—but on an earthplane level there was no change in the situation I had asked to heal.

Several years later during a Tarot reading (in September 1995) I asked why the situation hadn't changed. The reader showed me a series of past-life situations that had not been cleared, all of which were perspectives from lifetimes I was aware of but thought finished. As she talked about them, the Lords of Karma appeared to me again, still in black and looking quite formidable. They kept their arms crossed over their chests and said only one word, "Ask." As each situation came up in the reading, I asked to heal it. They said, "Granted" or "No." Even after the reading ended the Lords of Karma stayed. "Ask," they repeated. So I kept on asking all night.

They remained psychically present for days, and almost nonstop I asked for the healing and release of every pain and frustration I could think of in my life. Every item named suggested a dozen more. When I questioned the appropriateness of my asking for so much I was told again, "Ask." Remembering the first healer's warning about correct wording, I began to wonder if just "Granted" was enough. Through a series of questions to the Lords of Karma, I developed an inclusive list to ask for in each release that I hoped would fill in the loopholes. Thus the basic process was born. As time went on and the Lords of Karma became more talkative, I discovered ways to take the releases further into Core Soul healing. These evolved into the three extended processes.

After working with them for a week or so, I asked the Lords of Karma how long I would be able to continue receiving the dispensations, and if I could teach the process to others. I was

told that others could learn it, and that we could keep the opportunity until the next New Moon. At the next New Moon, the
Lords of Karma showed no signs of leaving, and when I asked
them they said I could continue until Hallows (October 31), a
month away. During that month, I did a workshop and asked if
I could teach the process. I was given no answer until the day of
the workshop and then told to do so. When I asked how long we
could use it, I was told until the first of the year. The workshop
group learned the routine readily and was excited by it. At the
first of the year I was told we could keep the process, and that I
could continue to teach it indefinitely.

A year later in early January, after teaching it in another
workshop and working privately with several women, I went to
bed and tuned into the Lords of Karma to thank them for their
help that day. I heard drumming and party sounds and asked,
"What's happening? Are you having a party up there?" The
reply was, "Yes, we're celebrating the end of karma." I had to
ask if I heard that correctly. "Why?" I wanted to know. "Critical
mass—enough people are doing it," was the reply. From that
night on, the Lords of Karma began appearing to me in white
robes with black collars and I could see their faces. Many in my
group were women, people of all races and skin colors. They
became very friendly, something they had never been before,
and far less scary to contact and work with.

Other people now perceive the Lords of Karma in this new
light; no one sees them now as austere and frightening. The
Lords of Karma have decided that we are using their gift wisely
and with respect, and they will continue to help us. If you don't
know how to phrase a question or know what to do next, ask
and they will tell you. You will still have to figure out for yourself what their directions mean. We may keep the process indefinitely for as long as karma still exists, and for as long as we
use it ethically and appropriately. They have decided that
karma can truly be ended on Earth, that we are ready to end it,
and they have chosen to support us in every way. However, do
not mistake their friendliness or playfulness; they are still all

powerful in our lives and lifetimes. Treat them always with the greatest respect and remember to thank them for the gift of each release.

Karma exists on Earth in four basic categories: relationships, situations, character traits, and dis-eases. All of these appear in this life and in other incarnations, though the basic process covers only the karma accrued on Earth. Every aspect of Earth karma will fit into one of these categories. Rather than working by categories, it is best to ask for help for everything and anything that is painful in your present life. By doing this, the relevant karmic patterns and past lives will surface along the way to be discovered and cleared. Because of the Earth changes and the plan for ascension of the planet, all unhealed karma from every past Earth incarnation is now manifesting in this life for the purpose of being completed.

Karmic release and healing are granted as grace or dispensation. This means that by recognizing that something in your life isn't working and needs healing, and by making the request in an appropriate way, the Lords of Karma will usually grant the release without further working out of the karma involved. The suffering ends by you asking for the release, and by having the request granted. The key here is recognizing what needs to be healed and what is beyond your own ability to release by simple choice and earthplane action. For example, if you know you don't look good wearing red, don't ask the Lords of Karma to heal it—just stop wearing red. But if you are experiencing abuse in a relationship and need help to extricate yourself from the relationship and pattern, the Lords of Karma will release the pattern (and from all of your lifetimes)—if you are willing to make the life and self-love changes required to do so.

While many situations change instantly, as soon as the request is granted, with some other requests you may be required to do further work. Dis-eases are a good example of this. Everyone thinks of dis-eases first when discussing karmic healing. However, to heal most dis-eases it is necessary to heal the more-than-physical causes of them. This may mean healing an abusive relationship or any other aspect of your life that is difficult and needs changing. When asking to clear a dis-ease, first ask to clear the emotional and situational difficulties in your life. Once those requests are granted, ask about the dis-ease. You may be given the release, or asked to do further work before it can be granted. A "no" response usually means further work is needed. Make requests to heal the painful situations, relationships, and character traits in your life first, then ask about the dis-ease again. It is also best to go beyond the basic process to clear serious dis-eases.

In all karmic healing, and particularly in the healing of relationships, be very clear that the only person you can change is yourself and the only releases you can ask for are for yourself. You may not ask to change other people without their direct participation and free choice, but you may ask to heal your small child or a pet. You can, however, heal a relationship by healing your part in it and that is usually enough to clear the situation. Your request might be worded, "I would like to heal my relationship with (name)." Or "I would like to heal my pattern of being abused in relationships."

Conflicted relationships usually bring to mind a mate, but they can also extend to difficult friendships, family members, children, co-workers, or bosses, etc. Often the source of difficulty in a relationship is something left over from a past life, or from a series of past lives. Look for this especially when the other person's animosity or conflict toward you seems inexplicable. When you start listing difficult relationships, you can go on for days. You must be specific in asking for release in each situation. Ask for karmic healing with everyone you can think of, people you know now and those you used to know, whether they are still alive or not. Ask to clear and heal your relationship with everyone in your life who has ever done you wrong or hurt you in any way. The worst of these will come to mind first. Doing this will heal a great deal of the present incarnation's karma and open up a lot of past lives besides.

There are several ways to ask for the karmic clearing of a

conflicted relationship. The first is to ask for *karmic healing* with the person or relationship. If the relationship is ended with that person, or if you wish for it to end, ask for *karmic release* as well. If the person is someone who has done you great wrong, either in a past life or the present, you may wish to ask for *karmic severance*. This is only for very serious situations and you must have the Lords of Karma's permission to ask for it before proceeding. Use this for your rapist, stalker, incest perpetrator, or someone who has had a pattern of killing you in past incarnations—only the heaviest stuff. For most active relationships, the request for karmic healing is enough. None of these requests violates the free will of the other person, but only expresses your will for the relationship itself.

Also ask for karmic healing for every peaceful and healthy relationship to smooth the path and keep it healthy and peaceful. Ask to heal your positive relationships with your mate, children, close friends, allies—all the loved and loving people in your life. You may get some interesting information about your past incarnations together and the relationships will be cleared of possible pitfalls before they happen. It is especially important for parents to heal their relationships with their children. There may be many significant lifetimes involved.

Situations are another category. For example, you may have worked hard all your life but are terribly poor and can't seem to get that one break that will free you. First, ask the Lords of Karma to release you from any past-life vows of poverty. These may have been positive at that time, but could be holding you back now. That done, ask to heal the situation and see what they tell you. Often the request is enough, and you will be ready to accept success and will receive it. Sometimes you may be directed to heal a past life with a similar situation, heal your ability or willingness to receive, or heal some negative interference. You will be told what to do, or you can ask what to do. Follow the directions you are given.

Character traits are a further aspect of karma. I had a pattern of yelling at frustrating strangers, often store clerks.

Friends would tease me about my Evil Elf coming out, and I was always horribly embarrassed and guilty. I asked to heal the pattern, but it didn't seem to change. One day, however, I asked to heal the Evil Elf. I was shown myself at about two years old, having a temper tantrum. I was quite abused as a child and apparently had split off a sub-personality in this way that resulted in the Evil Elf being formed. Imagine my dismay when I was told that she couldn't be healed. When I asked the Lords of Karma what to do next, they told me the Evil Elf had to go. I was frightened by their advice and asked them if it was for my highest good. They assured me that it was. I asked for it. My request was granted. When I woke up the next morning, I saw the Evil Elf heading upward, walking by herself and carrying a child's red suitcase. A doorway opened, she passed through it, and the door closed. I wasn't sorry, just relieved. I have never yelled unjustly at anyone again.

How you ask for karmic release is crucial. The question must be simply phrased and can encompass only one release at a time; be very careful that your wording is for what you wish to happen. Be careful what you ask for, you may get it. And since getting it will affect everything in your life, ask only for what you truly want and need. Word your requests so that they may be answered with a "yes" or "no." If you are familiar with a pendulum, the way you ask questions when you use it is the same as your requests of the Lords of Karma. If you receive a "no," try rewording it. Further information on releasing a "no" follows.

Ask for one release at a time. You may use the process as often as you want to, even repeating it for hours as I have often done, but do so with one question at a time. If you ask to heal your diabetes, clear your relationship with your mother, and meet your soul mate all in one request, you will have no way to track down a "no" response to release it or understand any further directions. The example above is actually three separate requests. To get meaningful responses and make the process manageable, ask these one at a time instead of all together.

Sometimes a request is denied. Arguing is the wrong thing to do in this case, and so is giving up. Instead, ask the Lords of Karma what you need to know or do to clear it. You will be given the information verbally or visually. Often the problem is from a past life, or a past (or present life) relationship that needs to be released. You may be shown the lifetime or situation, and you may or may not understand what you are being shown. Even if you don't understand it, ask to release it. Do this as a separate process. Once it's granted and the new process is finished, go back to your original question. This time the request is more likely to be a "yes." A past life that must be cleared first is the most frequent reason for refusal, and it is easily taken care of.

Sometimes there is something else to do, and the Lords of Karma will tell you what it may be. One woman, who asked to heal her recurrent breast cancer, was told that she had first to choose whether she wanted to live or not. She said she wasn't sure. The Lords of Karma told her to meditate on it and if she chose to stay, they would help her; if she chose to go, they would make it an easy death. I do not know what she decided. A woman who asked for a positive self-image was refused, and when she asked for advice she was told to request karmic severance with her date-rapist of many years ago. She did so and then went back to her first request, which was then granted.

Another woman asked to heal her liver dis-ease and was refused. She was told that she had to love herself more to have the healing. "Well, how do I do that?" she asked, but got no answer. I suggested she ask the Lords of Karma to *help* her to love herself more, and they agreed to do so. Another woman was directed to go to the beach more often. In another instance, a woman who asked for karmic healing with her dying husband was given a "no." When she asked what she needed to do, they told her to tell him that she loved him. Upon doing so, she made her original request again and it was granted. Most "no" responses can be cleared in these ways. In a few cases, the karma will not be released, and in some it will be released at a later time. If a request is a persistent "no," leave it and return to it from time to time. Something in the meantime may have changed the response. Also try the request again when you are familiar with the extended processes.

Karmic release work is individual work, self-healing in the deepest and most profound sense. It can be used ethically for other people only in very limited ways. When doing so be very sure not to violate the other person's free will or to manipulate her for your own gain or comfort. This is so even when you feel that your request is for her own good. To do so is a serious karma to accrue and a serious offense against ethics. The best way to use these processes for others is to teach the person how to do it themselves, and let them ask for whatever healing and karmic releases she may need. Only she can know what she really needs, as only you can know what you do.

If you still wish to ask help for someone who cannot or will not do it herself, karmic release can be done as a distance healing. Go into a meditative state and ask for the presence of the other person's Higher Self. Without her presence your request will be refused. If the Higher Self appears, ask her if she agrees to what you wish to ask for her. If she does, you may call in the Lords of Karma, tell them that you have her Higher Self's permission, and make your request. The Lords of Karma will then decide if you may proceed. If they agree, make the request in the Higher Self's presence and go through the steps of the process. You should always tell the person as soon as possible what you asked for and the response. This method may be used for small children and for pets, as well, who cannot verbally participate in the process. For more information on how to do distance healing, see my book *Psychic Healing with Spirit Guides and Angels* (The Crossing Press, 1996).

The basic Lords of Karma process goes further after your request is granted, to cover anything you may have missed and to make sure that the healing occurs on both the earthplane and higher energy soul levels. Healing that occurs only on the physical plane, or only beyond the physical plane, is not usually enough. For the healing to be permanent it must happen on emotional, mental, and spiritual levels as well, and the extended processes take the healing even further. Clearing your abused relationship on the physical level is important, but it is more important to remove the pattern of abuse from the emotional and mental levels and from all your past lifetimes. Otherwise, though the abusive relationship may end, another one may begin.

The process concludes by asking that the healing be done through all relevant lifetimes, and that the healing also manifest on Earth in the present. Releasing a present situation is helpful, but it may be more useful to release it at the source in the past life where it first began. It is also important to heal the situation in any other past lives where it occurred and where it may have contributed to the present situation. Equally important is to stipulate when you want the healing. To the Lords of Karma, and to most Be-ings who do not live on Earth, time is of no consequence. It doesn't exist where they are, but we have to live with it here on the material plane. A release that will happen someday is wonderful, but why not ask for it to happen NOW. If a situation or relationship needs healing, why wait?

The finishing request, used in all the Lords of Karma processes, reads as follows:

I ask for this healing
Through all the levels and all the bodies,
All the lifetimes, including the present lifetime,
Heal all the damage (from the situation),
And bring the healing into the present NOW.

You will use this to complete the process every time a request is granted. It covers a lot of bases, and even more bases are covered in the later extensions of the method.

If you receive a "yes" to the above, your request has been approved, and the process is done. There is no more to ask for. Say "Thank you." You may go on to another request or a series of requests. If the answer to a request is "no," ask the Lords of Karma what you need to do to get a "yes." Follow the directions they give you. You may also ask for this finishing request one line at a time, going forward with a "yes" and stopping to clear the "no" when you receive it. Other past lives may turn up, or the Lords of Karma may tell you that the healing can't be done now. If it can't, ask when. If you agree to the time lag, go ahead; if you don't agree, ask what can be done to speed it. Remember that even the partial healing of a major issue is a great improvement; the rest can be cleared later if necessary. If the healing is denied for a particular energy level or body, again ask what may be done to release the "no."

Most requests made to the Lords of Karma using these processes are granted but some may require the patience to unravel the no's. It is worth the patience and the additional work. You will learn a lot about yourself along the way. Always treat the Lords of Karma with the greatest respect, no matter how frustrated you may get. If you have difficulty in unraveling an issue, ask their help; they will usually give it to you and make the clearing easy. If asked, they may also suggest the proper wording or whatever is needed to make the process simple. Remember that these profound healers are on your side. They are here to help you with your soul growth and learning in any way that they may. They can only help you if you ask, and they can only release what you ask for. You are welcome to ask for as many releases, one at a time, as you wish, day or night. They never seem to sleep.

Making initial contact with the Lords of Karma is usually quite easy, and once you have made the contact it grows stronger and clearer with repetition. You do the process in a light meditative state, so your psychic senses can open to the information. If you have difficulty doing this, you may also ask the Lords of Karma to help you learn to work with them. Developing a clear working relationship is crucial for your healing; you must understand the information you are being given. People have a variety of psychic abilities and strengths and the Lords of Karma will usually convey information to you through your strongest psychic sense. If you are visual, you may see pictures—and may have to learn to interpret what you see. The pictures can be scenes or symbols, colors or flashes of light. You need to know which images mean a "yes" or "granted" and which represent a "no." If your psychic senses are auditory and you simply hear "yes" or "no," the process is even easier. If you then don't hear a response, tell them you can't hear them and ask that it be repeated until you understand it.

If you are visual and don't understand the colors or images you see, ask the Lords of Karma to show you a "yes" response. When you understand what that is, ask to see a "no." Sometimes a "no" is no response at all, while "yes" might be a bright color or a flash of light. One woman who receives information visually sees the Lords of Karma in black robes for a "no" and white ones for a "yes." One woman sees the color red for her "no" and green for "yes"—a karmic traffic light. Another sees red for her "yes" and nothing at all for "no." It may take some work to translate such symbols, but they will become clear with a little thought.

The contact with the Lords of Karma is usually very gentle, such as subtle changes on the visual field of your closed eyes. Any response is a contact, a change of light, a color. Other senses may be involved, that of feeling or even fragrance. "Yes" may be a sense of peace or relief, or warmth in the body, or the fragrance of roses, rather than a sound or image. One student feels a "yes" response as comfort in her heart, and a "no" as discomfort in her solar plexus. Everyone's psychic senses are different; you must learn to pay attention to subtle changes and interpret them. A quiet meditative state is best when you are first making contact and learning to understand the responses. Once you are proficient you can probably do it anywhere. Don't do it while driving, however, as the trance is deeper and may take longer than you realize.

For those few people in my workshops who are unable to make contact with the Lords of Karma in the ways I have outlined, I recommend that they buy or make a pendulum and learn how to use it. If asked, the Lords of Karma will work through a pendulum. It can be any small weight at the end of a few inches of string or light chain. A necklace pendant will usually work. To be accurate and useful, however, pendulums must be kept cleared by placing them in a bowl of salt or under a pyramid every night and when they are not being used. If you use pendulums frequently, it is best to have several, so they are always cleared and ready. An uncleared pendulum will not give accurate responses, and may just swing erratically.

To use a pendulum, you must first determine its "yes" and "no" responses; these are transmitted through your nervous system. To do this, hold the end of the chain steady in your dominant hand, allowing the weight to swing. Clear your mind of all extraneous thoughts, then ask the pendulum to "show you a yes." In a few moments the pendulum will swing, seemingly by itself. Ask to see a "no" in the same way. With a little practice you will become familiar with "yes" and "no" and recognize the responses easily. Now ask if the Lords of Karma would be willing to run the pendulum for you. You should see your "yes" response (otherwise the pendulum probably needs to be cleared). If you ask then if you have made contact through the pendulum with the Lords of Karma, you will usually receive a "yes" again.

Ask for your first karmic release, using the responses of the pendulum to advise you of the "yes" and "no" responses of the process. Always when you begin, ask to make sure it is really the Lords of Karma running the pendulum. If it is not, ask whoever is there to leave, then ask for the Lords of Karma again. Proceed only when you know you have the contact. This is a little different from the usual way of doing the Lords of Karma processes, but it works quite well.

Whether using a pendulum or psychic response, once you have made initial contact and know how to assess an answer as "yes" and "no," you may begin to make requests for karmic release. Most people learn this within a few minutes in my workshops. If you have not made clear contact, continue trying until you do, as you cannot go further otherwise. Ask for help from the Lords of Karma themselves if you need it. Most people who tell me they have not made contact actually have done so but don't recognize it. Any response at all, no matter how subtle, is a contact. Look within and pay attention to what you perceive.

Also avoid trying too hard, as this is the best way to miss the responses totally. Relax and enjoy the process and enjoy your meeting with these Ascended Be-ings. They will make every effort to reach you and to work with you. They have your highest good and greatest healing in their hearts, and your sincere effort is usually all that is needed. I have taught several children to work with the Lords of Karma and they do it easily. Anyone can do this, and openness with positive intent is usually all that's needed to ensure success.

The Lords of Karma have been waiting for a long time to be able to release us and the Earth from our karmic sufferings and entanglements. Just give them the chance and they will do it. The more you work with these Be-ings, the more amazed you will be at the changes and healing they bring to your life. The processes are simple and profound. It will be a long time before you run out of things to ask for to heal your life.

Now that you have made contact with the Lords of Karma and understand their "yes" and "no" responses, it is time to begin using the Basic Process of karmic release.

I. The Basic Process

When I teach the Lords of Karma Basic Process to groups or individuals, here is how I begin. I ask them to get relaxed and quiet, close their eyes, and enter a light meditative state. Then I tell them to ask to speak with the Lords of Karma. After a minute or two I ask, "Is there anyone who has not made the contact?" Those few people raise their hands. When I ask those who haven't if they experienced anything at all, most have received some impression. It may simply be a feeling of presence. People who are visual describe seeing colors, Light, picture images or symbols, or seeing the Lords of Karma themselves come forward. Those who are auditory hear the responses and may enter conversation with the Masters. Some people experience body sensations or fragrances. All are authentic contacts and all convey the required information.

Next I lead the group through a request that everyone agrees to. Since my groups are primarily all women, a good beginning is to have everyone ask for positive self-image. This is the first of the Universals that appear throughout the Lords of Karma processes. Universals are things to ask for that everyone seems to need. I recommend asking for them, as most or all will be useful to you. Other Universals for this Basic Process include: asking for release from negative interference on all levels, and asking for *gentle* release of all heart scars. A further important request is to ask to bring your life's focus into living in the present.

Negative interference is an issue that will be repeated in a variety of ways throughout the Lords of Karma and Essential Energy Balancing® systems. Evil and manipulation exist in the world and are real. When you are granted this release, you may be amazed at the images that came with it. Before asking to release heart scars—old emotional heart pain that blocks openness and your ability to love—realize that a heart scar clearing can be painful. The clearing may not happen immediately, but usually within three days. You may awake one morning in great heart-area pain, which can seem physical but is not. Fear, anguish, and flashbacks of old hurts may come with the pain. The entire incident can last for up to an hour. Once a heart scar is cleared, however, you will experience new freedom and joy. Heart scars exist on the emotional body level. An uncleared heart scar becomes pain carried into other lifetimes, that is, karma.

Another Universal request is to live in the present. Women in particular tend to focus too much on the past, reliving old hurts that are long since ended. When these hurts are finished, you can move forward and begin to live in the now. Many people also focus on living in the future (some live in past and future both, avoiding the now totally). They see their life as something that will come, that hasn't happened yet, but will be wonderful later. However, later tends to move further and further away. Living in the past, or waiting for your life to begin in some future that never comes, prevents joyful living in the now. As you move further into the ascension process, you will find that the past is healed by the Lords of Karma (if you have done your work) and the future is created by the present and will take care of itself. Now is where we are and is all that matters; make the most of it.

Taking students through the Universals teaches the Basic Process. By the time they have experienced the first request in full, they have met the Lords of Karma, learned to ask for a karmic release, understood the response, and experienced the finishing process (all the levels, and all the bodies, etc.). I ask at each step, "If anyone receives a 'no' raise your hand," and work with those people to clear it. Most "no" responses will clear easily, as previously described. Sometimes just making the request again brings the "yes" response. By the time the group has gone through two or three requests, they understand the process.

Next, I tell the group to "Ask for karmic healing for the relationship of your choice. If anyone receives a 'no,' raise your hand." Again, I work with those receiving "no's" until they clear them. If there is time, I lead the group through the process three more times—to release a situation, a character trait, and physical condition of their choice. I ask them to do more releases later, after the workshop ends. Try all of these for yourself now, using the full process outlined below. By the time you have completed these releases, you will be well on your way to healing your present life and all your unhealed past lifetimes on Earth.

Because you are now sufficiently familiar with the process to ask for anything you need, you can keep going. Everyone has suffering in this life—it is the nature of living. You will find innumerable things to ask the Lords of Karma to heal. You may work days just on healing negative relationships and days longer when you ask to clear the positive ones. The things you need most will come to your mind immediately; you may have already asked for them just reading this far. This system was given to us to be used—use it thoroughly and often to heal all that troubles and restricts your life and joy. Consider the Lords of Karma angelic realm agents of the Goddess Source, as the best friends you will ever meet. Remember to thank them and appreciate them. Once you are thoroughly familiar with working with the Lords of Karma, teach the process to others for their healing as well.

Once a Basic Process request is granted, the changes happen immediately; with the extended levels it takes a bit longer. You may only be aware that the request was granted—you may not feel any different, but the change is there. The next time the situation arises, or you encounter the person, or get medically checked for the dis-ease, you may discover that the problem no longer exists or that the situation has changed considerably for the better. It happens so naturally that you may not even remember that the change came from your request to the Lords of Karma.

Occasionally a detoxification reaction occurs. This happens particularly if you do a great number of releases over a short period of time. However, even then the detoxification is brief and rarely difficult or uncomfortable. Some detox symptoms include sleeping a lot, restlessness, depression, diarrhea, frequent or heavy urination, feeling hot, hot sweats, a cold or runny nose, or flu symptoms. Despite the symptoms you will still feel very well, and the symptoms rarely last longer than a few days. These symptoms are a physical cleansing that you need. Don't use medicines to stop them. Drink lots of water with a slice of lemon in it while they are happening.

You may also experience flashbacks, old movies of past painful incidents. Simply watch them moving through. There may or may not be emotions attached, but the emotions and the scenes pass very quickly. Don't fight these, or try to shut them out. Consider them as pain leaving and just let them happen. Do not hesitate to ask for multiple Lords of Karma releases in fear of these detoxifications, as they are an easy price to pay for the gift they have granted you.

If a karmic issue is a simple one, or only involves one simple past-life situation, the Basic Process is probably enough to heal it completely. However, if your issue is more major, for a serious dis-ease or long-term karmic pattern, you will wish to use the extended processes along with the basic release. Once you have learned the three processes that follow this first Lords of Karma method, use them to repeat the more serious of the healings you have already done with this first step. You may ask the Lords of Karma with each request if using the extended processes is needed.

Once you begin working with the Lords of Karma, ideas for the requests you need to make will come to you at all hours of the day and night. This is important information which can be lost very quickly. It seems to happen frequently that a request not asked for immediately is forgotten within a few moments. There are two ways to handle this. One is to do the request as soon as the idea occurs to you, or you can write a reminder to do it later. If you don't do one or the other of these, the idea may be lost—and the karmic release you lose may be an important key to your healing.

Here is the Basic Lords of Karma Process. Begin working with it and with the Lords of Karma now.

WORKING WITH THE LORDS OF KARMA

I. The Basic Process

1. Ask to speak with the Lords of Karma. You will receive some perception of them.

2. Ask for the release you wish.

3. You will perceive a "yes" or "no" answer.

4. If the answer is "yes," ask to have the release

   Through all the levels and all the bodies,
   All the lifetimes including the present lifetime,
   Heal all the damage (from the situation),
   And bring the healing into the present NOW.

   If the answer is "yes," the process is finished.

5. If the answer to your question is "no," ask what you need to know or do to have the release and wait for the response.

   If you are shown a past life or something else that you do or don't understand, ask to clear and release what you are seeing. You will get a "yes" or "no" answer—if "yes," do #4.

   If "no," ask again, "What do I need to clear, know, or do to release it?"

   Once you get a "yes" to releasing the obstacle, go back to your original question and ask again. You will likely get a "yes." Do #4 to finish.

6. If you get a "no" to #4, ask for a "yes" or "no" to each phrase. When you find the "no," do #5.

7. You may ask as many questions at one time, as often as you wish. Keep the questions very simple, one request at a time.

8. Use this process on four categories of karmic healing:

   a. to heal dis-eases or physical conditions

   b. to heal conflicted relationships of all types

c. to heal negative personality traits or habits

d. to heal negative life situations

9. Treat these Be-ings with great respect, never argue with them, and say thank you.

Universal healings: Do these one at a time. Ask for positive self-image, release from negative interference on all levels, and gentle release of all heart scars. Ask to bring your focus into present time.

II. The Outer Levels

Taking karmic release to the Outer Levels moves the healing further into your Core Soul energy. Some karmic issues are not simple incidents from this life or from a single past lifetime, but are recurring patterns through your many incarnations. Pain that is not healed in the lifetime of its source may be carried forward into other lives until it is healed or released. The pain may be compounded by the repetition and complication through many incarnations. An emotional hurt not healed moves through the energy levels, becoming entrenched more deeply in your energy. The hurt moves into the mental body, where if still unhealed it moves into the spiritual body. Since physical, emotional, mental, and spiritual levels all have higher octaves of energy bodies that mirror them, the entrenchment of pain can become complex and deep. Simple healing is not enough when this occurs, and it occurs frequently.

The physical body's next energy octave is the etheric level, and the emotional body's next octave is the astral level. The Mind Grid is the mental body's higher octave and is the place where karma is programmed into one's energy system. The spiritual body has higher octaves in the galactic and causal body levels, and there are many spiritual bodies beyond these levels. Each of these higher bodies—the etheric, astral, Mind Grid, galactic, and causal bodies—contains a consciousness of its own that is a higher octave of Be-ing. These consciousness levels are the Energy Selves that will be discussed (and met) later in Essential Energy Balancing®. When karmic trauma reaches these higher energy octaves, it affects every aspect of your life in ways you may never realize. These outer octaves also have to be healed to free your Energy Selves to rejoin with you.

The Outer Level karmic release process is designed to clear these further bodies. It is used for major healing issues, and for issues that have not cleared with the Basic Process after a reasonable length of time. It can be used to heal your karmic contract pre-life agreements about an issue, and to rewrite your Akashic Record. Outer Level release also heals aspects of a request that may be more than karmic, as in DNA or Core Soul damage. The extended process heals damage or traumas that may have occurred when you were not incarnated in a body—damage that happened between lifetimes, for example. Unlike the Basic Process, Outer Level healing can release damage from incarnations on other planets.

From just these brief descriptions, you may begin to realize how complex our lives, lifetimes, and energy structures are. With the Outer Level process, the request to the Lords of Karma is extended through four new items. These items move quickly, as there is rarely a "no" to these—unless the request for that level is not needed. If you receive a "no," ask if the release is needed through that level. If it is not, just go on. Only if you are told "no," and told that the release at that point is necessary, must you go through the steps for clearing it. To do this, ask the Lords of Karma what you need to know or do to have the release at that level and follow their directions. As in the Basic Process, if they show you something that needs to be healed, go through the process of healing it.

In order for the Outer Level healings to occur, you must have reconnected your twelve-strand DNA. This is done in the first Essential Energy Balancing® process, but you may also do it immediately by making it a request to the Lords of Karma. Use the Outer Level process when doing this. Once you have learned to use the four simple requests that heal the Outer Levels, you will use this extended process for all requests, unless the Lords of Karma tell you that release on Outer Levels is unnecessary.

The four Outer Levels are: the Mind Grid level, DNA level,

Karmic Contract level, and the Core Soul level and beyond. Simple definitions of these follow. The Mind Grid is the outer octave of the mental body, the place where karma is programmed into human and animal energy. It looks like a domed gold screen or mesh and contains all of the consensus realities of the planet and your culture. All of the beliefs of Earth, your country, and your family are programmed into the Mind Grid via the DNA by the time of birth. These basic beliefs are compounded by everything you learn, correctly or incorrectly, from birth on. These belief systems can be highly difficult to change, but often changing them is vital for your continued growth.

For example, if you grew up in a family who taught you that other races were inferior, you may have to work now to change that false belief. The Mind Grid is basically a computer. It has no feelings or emotions, only thought forms, thought processes, and ideas. Like a computer, it can be programmed: old programming can be changed,\if you know how to do it. Asking for karmic release through the Mind Grid level is a way of reprogramming the karmic computer, literally changing your mind.

Neurological defects can reflect damage or tears in the Mind Grid. If you are dyslexic, for example, you may have a Mind Grid with tears and holes in it, knots, or pulled and broken wires in the mesh. Asking for healing through the Mind Grid level may affect the nervous system, and can possibly result in physical healing. This is the level for you to go to for releasing stroke damage, visual difficulties, and dis-eases of the mind and brain. While no one can promise physical cures, you may be surprised at the amount of healing (different from physical medicine) that can occur. It is positive for everyone to go to the Lords of Karma and ask to heal their Mind Grid—use the Outer Level process to do so.

The DNA level is next. The DNA is the code directing what we look like, who we become, and how our cells and organs grow. DNA carries, however, more than our physical characteristics. It carries all the directions to form and heal our energy bodies, levels, chakras, and systems—all of our nonphysical anatomy, including our mental and spiritual structures and the programming of the Mind Grid. It also carries the programming of the karma we incarnate with. For a permanent change to occur in many karmic release issues, the DNA must be reprogrammed, reconnected, and healed.

Most of the instructions for our spiritual evolution are excluded from the two-strand DNA we currently carry. Life on Earth began with twelve DNA strands, not two, but the other five pairs were disconnected not so long ago. Our full energy complement beyond our Earth incarnations contains twenty-one DNA strands, and there are a total of thirty-eight! These may be reconnected when we achieve ascension. Earth has been the focus of interplanetary war since its inception, and the disconnection of Earth DNA was a casualty of that war. It happened at about the same time that patriarchy took control over the Goddess cultures. Most people believe that happened over ten thousand years ago, but I believe it to be more recent, within three thousand years.

Because our full complement of DNA has been disconnected (not destroyed), it can be reconnected, clearing the way for major healing on all levels and for the vital expansion of our abilities. With your full complement of DNA, your psychic abilities will increase significantly. Reconnection also makes possible the clearing of the more than fifty percent or more of our karma necessary for ascension and also the energy changes that occur with ascension itself.

Our Karmic Contracts are the agreements made between each individual and the Lords of Karma before birth. These agreements are carefully thought through, agreed to, and devised with maximum soul growth in mind. However, we are programmed to forget these agreements at the time we are born. Working with the Lords of Karma is nothing new to us: we have done so countless times in numerous pre-lifetimes. Much of our suffering that needs releasing with the Lords of Karma has been scripted into this lifetime's Karmic Contracts.

These contracts can be revised—they are being revised and

rewritten continually. To release a situation from the Karmic Contract requires completion of the required learning. Asking for the healing on the Karmic Contract level provides the learning necessary for the release. The karmic record of all of a soul's many incarnations is called the Akashic Record. Release of an issue through the Karmic Contract level also revises the Akashic Record for all relevant lifetimes for that issue.

The last of the four Outer Levels is the Core Soul level and beyond. I define the Core Soul as all energy above the physical, emotional, and mental bodies. This includes the next higher octave, which contains the etheric body, astral body, and Mind Grid, plus all of the spiritual bodies and levels (there are many of these). Our energy is composed of numerous reflecting octaves and layers of bodies and levels, chakra systems, template doorways, and the nonphysical wiring to connect them all. Releasing karma from the closer-to-physical levels is relatively easy, and most of our this-life karma is contained there. However, we are barely aware of the many additional components of who we are. Asking for healing on the Core Soul level and beyond carries the release much more deeply through our very complex energy systems.

What must usually be healed at these levels is Core Soul damage, rather than karma per se. Unhealed soul damage carries forward from lifetime to lifetime. The damage can occur when the soul is formed and separated from the Light/Goddess or any time thereafter. It is usually damage to the energy levels themselves rather than to the physical body, damage that often occurs between lifetimes. Negative interference can be a source of Core Soul damage. Sometimes it simply comes from being in the wrong place at the wrong time, with no karmic meaning. Most of us incarnated now on Earth have had many lifetimes and we are carrying some element of Core Soul damage in our energy makeup. A large part of Essential Energy Balancing® is directed at healing that damage.

There is an interesting list of Universal healings at these Outer Levels. Probably the most vital one is to ask the Lords of

Karma to release you from emotional starvation. When you get a "yes," ask for the healing through the four extended levels (Mind Grid, DNA, Karmic Contract, Core Soul level and beyond), and then finish with "All the levels, and all the bodies, etc." This is an extremely powerful healing for almost everyone. Emotional starvation is a central karma in many Earth incarnations. Ask also to heal feeling inadequate, negative thinking, the need for material things or a particular person to feel whole, and all negative excesses in your life. Doing these will clear some major Earth suffering and teach you to use the Outer Level process.

For a further Universal healing, ask the Lords of Karma to clear, heal, and release you gently of all negative cords and hooks on all levels. Use this precise wording. Take the healing through the Outer Levels and through all the levels and all the bodies, etc., to finish. Clear any "no" responses as in the Basic Process. If the "no" is in one of the Outer Levels, however, ask if the release is needed there before trying to clear it. If you don't need release at that level, just go on to the next.

Negative cords are connections of other people's energy to your chakras that can occur on any body level. People will connect to you to draw upon your energy, consciously or not. They may want something from you, need something from you, or simply drain you because they don't know how to stand on their own energetically. There may be many people pulling at you, and some may be people you don't even know. Clearing these cords can make the person being disconnected angry for a while. However, releasing these cords does no harm to them and does you much good. At those times when you feel weighted down by life or responsibility, try this karmic release. Because cords tend to keep returning, clearing them needs to be done periodically.

Negative hooks are significant karmic attachments to people on the emotional body level or higher. These are karmic connections from other lifetimes, brought in at birth. They do a great deal of harm. Hooks are often obstructions to your life energy or to the fulfillment of your life path. The people attaching to you in this way are often those who are causing you harm in this life and have caused you harm before. Removing negative hooks can result in emotional and physical relief and release. If you have chronic fatigue syndrome, look for these hooks and ask the Lords of Karma to remove them gently. Hooks usually have to be removed only once.

Another Universal healing through the Outer Levels is to ask the Lords of Karma to heal, return, and reintegrate all soul fragments on all levels. Again, take the healing through the Outer Levels, and through all the levels, and all the bodies, etc. At times of strong emotional pain, the Astral Twin/Inner Child can suffer damage. Fragments that are holograms of your Astral Twin break off and float free, making you feel spacey, disconnected, emotionally numb, disinterested in life, and just not all there. With the many incarnations we have experienced, and the many traumas incurred in them, the Astral Twin can be fragmented into many pieces. Asking for this healing returns the healed pieces to your energy field.

This healing will not happen immediately or all at once but can take a period of months. Piece by piece the fragments return. You will feel them as a warmth entering your heart, usually at times when you are totally relaxed between sleep and waking. Returning these fragments feels very good, and you will feel better in every way as the pieces reconnect and come together.

While you are asking the Lords of Karma for Inner Child healing, try one more Universal request. Ask the Lords of Karma to reprogram your Inner Child/Astral Twin for full health and wholeness. Again, take the healing through the four Outer Levels, and finish with all the levels and all the bodies, etc. Healing your Astral Twin is necessary to enter ascension, and more healing happens for her in Essential Energy Balancing®.

This second Lords of Karma process is simply an addition of four requests to the Basic Process. Once you receive a "yes" to your request, ask for the healing through the Mind Grid level,

DNA level, Karmic Contract level, and the Core Soul level and beyond. Finish the process by asking for the healing:

Through all the levels and all the bodies,
All the lifetimes including the present lifetime,
Heal all the damage (from the situation),
And bring the healing into the present NOW.

If you receive a "no," clear it by asking what you need to know or do to release it, and asking for karmic release of any hang-ups. Remember to thank the Lords of Karma after each process.

WORKING WITH THE LORDS OF KARMA

II. The Outer Levels

1. Ask to speak with the Lords of Karma. You will receive some perception of them.

2. Ask for the release you wish.

3. You will perceive a "yes" or "no" answer.

4. If the answer is "yes," ask to have the release through each of the Outer Levels listed below.

   If the answer is "no," proceed with the original process, the Lords of Karma Process I, and return to this point when you have a "yes."

   Then ask for the healing through:
   a. the Mind Grid level
   b. the DNA level
   c. the Karmic Contract (or Akashic Record) level
   d. the Core Soul level and beyond

   If the answer is "no" to any of these, ask if the healing is needed at that level—it may not be and, if not, go on. If the answer is "no" and release is needed, ask what to do to proceed.

5. When you have a "yes" to all of the Outer Levels, ask for the healing:

   Through all the levels and all the bodies,
   All the lifetimes including the present lifetime,
   Heal all the damage (from the situation),
   And bring the healing into the present NOW.

   If the answer is "yes," the process is finished. Say thank you.

6. If the answer is "no," proceed with the original process to clear the "no."

7. Use this Outer Level process for:
   a. major healing issues
   b. issues that have not cleared with the original process after a reasonable length of time
   c. to heal your Karmic Contract pre-life agreements
   d. healing that may be more than karmic, as in DNA or Core Soul damage
   e. healing of damage or traumas that may have occurred when you were not incarnated in a body
   f. healing of damage from incarnation on other planets

Universal healings: release emotional starvation, feeling inadequate, codependency, negative thinking, "I can't thinking," all negative cords and hooks. Ask to heal, return, and fully integrate all soul fragments. Release your need for material objects or a particular person to feel whole and satisfied, heal all negative excess in your life, and reprogram your Inner Child/Astral Twin for health and wholeness.

III. The Furthest Reaches

A very few situations have been with you since your soul was formed. The Moment of Self is the point at which your "self" differentiates from the Light Beyond the Goddess. It is the birth of the soul, of who you are. The center of the Earth is the point of your soul's connection to all of its incarnations on this planet. Connection to the center of the Earth is what makes us belong to this planet for the time of our being here, through all of our Earth lifetimes. It makes the Earth our home.

Though these "places" seem very far away and external to us, they are part of our energy and actually within us. The Moment of Self is anchored in our hearts and all of our Be-ing radiates outward from it. Think of it as a circle or, more properly, a spiral, instead of a line moving far away. The center of the Earth is anchored in our feet, and all the energy bodies have chakras in the feet that reach for the Earth's center. The planet's center is actually our own.

A healing that reaches from below the center of the Earth to beyond the Moment of Self incorporates everything in our energy, top to bottom, side to side, in and out, around and around—all the levels and components of our Be-ing. Sometimes it takes all of that to heal a karmic situation, pattern of suffering, or damage to our energy. Requesting that the healing occur from below the center of the Earth to beyond the Moment of Self leaves no stone or energy component uncovered in the healing. The Furthest Reaches actually go deepest into the spiral of energy that is who we are. Ask for this healing only with the Lords of Karma's permission. Not many releases require it. If the request is refused, do not attempt to clear the "no."

Occasionally, when something significant needs to be cleared that has very negative energy, you may be directed to use this request in the opposite direction. You would then ask for the healing from beyond your Moment of Self to below the center of the Earth. If you receive a "no" to the first request, ask if the healing needs to be done reversed. If the answer is still "no," finish the process without trying to clear the "no."

Before you can do healing through the center of the Earth, you must be fully connected into it. This is done in the first Essential Energy Balancing® process (along with the twelve strand DNA reconnection), but may also be done as a request to the Lords of Karma. Be sure to extend the request through the Outer Levels. Ask the Lords of Karma to extend and reconnect your grounding system into and through the center of the Earth. You will feel stronger and more stable in daily life for doing this. The request will not prevent you from astral traveling or psychically leaving your body, but instead makes both traveling and returning more secure. With this anchor you can go further and more safely.

There are some significant Universals with this extension of the Lords of Karma process. First of all, repeat the Outer Level healings for removing negative cords and hooks on all levels, and for healing, returning, and reintegrating all soul fragments. Ask for them from below the center of the Earth to beyond the Moment of Self. This will complete these healings through every part of your energy and Be-ing. Ask to release all abuse given or received and take the healing to the Furthest Reaches. Remember to ask for the release through the Outer Levels, and finish by asking for it through all the levels and all the bodies, etc.

Some other Universal healings from below the center of the Earth to beyond the Moment of Self include asking to be healed of judgment on all levels, to release disempowerment on all levels, and to heal and release abandonment. Ask for complete energy healing and Core Soul healing on all levels. Ask to release all negative karmic implants, and to heal all life force disruption through all the levels and components of your Be-ing. Profound changes and releases happen with these healings, life-changing transformations of all types. You will find healing for things you didn't know you needed, but that are vitally important with these clearings. Add to these Universals your own individual karmic situations.

Unlike the Basic Process, karmic releases through the Outer Levels and Moment of Self do not happen instantly. It takes at least three weeks for these healings to be felt on physical levels. Detoxification symptoms are possible with these extended processes. After my first requests to heal from the center of the Earth to the Moment of Self, I experienced about five days of lethargy and depression. When such reactions occur, treat yourself gently and understand that they are part of the clearing process and will pass. Sleep more if you need to, nurture yourself with chocolate or ice cream, and just wait for them to end. Karmic release that extends throughout your soul is worth a few days of discomfort. It may take some time until you realize just how profound the healing has been. Remember to thank the Lords of Karma for these gifts.

WORKING WITH THE LORDS OF KARMA

III. The Furthest Reaches

Use this process only after becoming thoroughly familiar with working with the Lords of Karma processes I and II.

Begin to use this process immediately, with and following processes I and II, for all serious and urgent karmic issues.

1. Complete Lords of Karma processes I and II, achieving a "yes" through the Core Soul level and beyond.

2. Ask the Lords of Karma to grant your question/release:

   FROM BELOW THE CENTER OF THE EARTH TO BEYOND YOUR MOMENT OF SELF

   It is necessary to use the exact above wording.

3. If the answer is "yes," ask for the healing:

Through all the levels and all the bodies,
All the lifetimes including the present lifetime,
Heal all the damage (from the situation),
And bring the healing into the present NOW.

4. If the answer is "yes," the process is finished.

   Expect the clearing to take approximately three weeks. Say thank you.

5. If the answer is "no," ask if the request is to be made in the opposite direction, from beyond the Moment of Self to below the center of the Earth. If the answer is still "no," do not try to change it. This request is not needed for all releases.

If you are doing processes I, II, and III at one session:

1. Contact the Lords of Karma.

2. State your request. If the answer is "no," proceed as in process I until you have achieved a "yes."

3. When the answer is "yes," ask to have the healing through each of the following:
   a. the Mind Grid level
   b. the DNA level
   c. the Karmic Contract/Akashic Record level
   d. the Core Soul level and beyond

   If the answer is "no" to any of these, ask if the healing is needed at that level. It may not be, and if not, go on. If the answer is "no" and a release is needed, ask what is needed to proceed.

4. When you have a "yes" to all of the above, ask for the healing or release **from below the center of the Earth to beyond your Moment of Self.**

5. If the answer is "yes," ask for the healing:

   Through all the levels and all the bodies,
   All the lifetimes including the present lifetime,
   Heal all the damage (from the situation),
   And bring the healing into the present NOW.

6. If the answer is "yes," say thank you. Expect the clearing to take approximately three weeks.

7. If the answer is "no," ask if you need the release in the opposite direction, from beyond the Moment of Self to below the center of the Earth. If so, proceed accordingly. If not, finish the process without trying to clear the "no."

Be aware of the seriousness of what you have just done; these healing will change your life and lifetimes—past, present, and future—forever. Be extremely careful in what you ask for and aware of the gift you are being given.

Universal healings: release all abuse given or received from below the center of the Earth to beyond your Moment of Self. Heal judgment on all levels, release personal disempowerment on all levels, and heal and release abandonment. Ask for complete energy healing, Core Soul healing, and the healing, return, and full integration of all soul fragments (repeat this again). Release all negative karmic implants, all negative cords and hooks (repeat), all karma with evil, and heal all life force disruption on all levels.

IV. Sealing Unto the Light

To seal something unto the Light and unto protection (of the Goddess) forever is to hard-wire it into your Core Soul, not only for this lifetime and this planet, but for all the lifetimes and all the planets you may ever incarnate upon. It includes the past, present, and future. Forever is a very long time, so be very sure that anything you ask to be sealed in this way is something you really want to keep. Only a very few healings require this final Lords of Karma process.

This is a method to use only by direct permission of the Lords of Karma—ask them before you even make the request. It will be granted only for a few healings. Try this process only after you are fully familiar with the basic and extended Lords of Karma releases and have done many of them for yourself. You should be very familiar with working with the Lords of Karma by this time, and have a cooperative relationship with your Lords of Karma group. If your request to seal a release unto the Light and unto protection forever is refused, do not try to clear the "no." Finish your request through all the levels and all the bodies, etc.

Sealing unto the Light is used only for things you wish to keep, karmic gifts too precious to ever lose again. Use it for such requests as complete Core Soul healing or permanent energy protection on all levels. (These are two Universals for this process.) Do not use it for anything you have asked to be cleared, removed, or healed from your energy or your life. What you wish to have taken away is not to be sealed unto the Light.

You will not ask for sealing unto the Light for anything nega-tive. For example, do not ask for it in a release of negative interference. You might, however, ask that your energy *once cleared* of negative interference be sealed unto the Light and unto protection forever. This is a method for adding to your positive karma, rather than releasing what has been negative.

My first requests for sealing unto the Light and unto protection forever were to offer my will and my healing hands to the Goddess. I asked for the healing fully, completely, permanently, and forever through the Basic Process, through the Outer Levels and Moment of Self, and asked that the healing be sealed unto the Light. The request was granted and I felt filled with a deep joy and peace for doing it. If you wish to do so, use the process to dedicate yourself to the Light and to the Goddess/God/Source of your choice. Be aware of the seriousness of the request; it is a permanent karmic vow that may be irrevocable.

Despite its seriousness, or perhaps because of it, sealing unto the Light can be used for some Universal healings. All of the following have only the most positive karmic consequences and are great gifts to receive if the Lords of Karma grant them. I have already mentioned asking for complete Core Soul healing and permanent energy protection on all levels. Ask also to forgive yourself and all others, and seal the forgiveness unto the Light and unto protection forever. Ask to know that you deserve to have good things in your life. Many people feel they don't deserve good things in their lives, thus preventing their karmic freedom and healing. Ask for positive self-love, the source of all love and union in one's life.

Use the full karmic process and sealing unto the Light and unto protection forever to bring in and integrate all alternate realities. These are lifetimes we live simultaneously on multiple, different dimensions. Sometimes a healing cannot be completed because an alternate reality prevents it; something different is happening for you there than is happening here and the realities have to be reconciled. In an ascension process, all of these multiple realities are brought in and integrated into one, just as all soul fragments are integrated into your astral body.

Some healers believe that alternate realities are a variety of soul fragment, a split-off of truths where possibilities contradict. The concept is complex. If the idea that there are many of you on many dimensions makes you dizzy, this request of the Lords of Karma will remedy the situation. After it is granted, you may experience some very strange dreams for a few weeks, until the alternate realities are brought in. My dreams seemed violent and frightening, and I was glad when the realities were finally cleared.

Another great gift to ask for with sealing unto the Light is to be reunited with your soul family. Today's healers on Earth are the troubleshooters of the Universe. We take combat assignment on many planets to heal seemingly impossible situations. We leave our homes, which are not on Earth, and we leave the people we most truly love. Like women who create their families from chosen loving friends instead of from their birth families, we healers have our soul families from Home. Some of the members may be with us in this lifetime, but most are not. It is the greatest gift to be reunited with those of our family who are on Earth with us, and whom we may not yet know in this incarnation. It is an even greater gift to be granted permanent reunion, not to be separated from our families for assignments again.

Asking for this healing can have wonderful consequences. If you have ever been lonely on Earth, you are missing your soul family. The granting of this request begins to bring them to you. Suddenly there are new people in your life, a loving support system that you've always longed for but never had before. You meet your true soul mate. You are no longer isolated from other healers. You no longer feel yourself a freak among people who have no understanding of who you are. People who are like you come into your life. So many of us are isolated—this request to the Lords of Karma ends that loneliness forever. You are beginning a process of ascension which will make you even more different from those around you. The loving support of your soul family is more important now than ever before.

Requests made to seal a healing unto the Light and unto protection forever take about three weeks to manifest. Some requests may take longer. Few detoxification or release symptoms seem to come with this healing. Sealing unto the Light is the ultimate blessing of the Goddess.

WORKING WITH THE LORDS OF KARMA

IV. Sealing Unto the Light

Use this process only after becoming thoroughly familiar with Lords of Karma processes I–III. This continues the healing for a very few requests only.

Use it for healings that are gifts granted that you wish to become part of your karma forever: beyond this lifetime, through all lifetimes—past, present, and future—and including and beyond the Moment of Self. It is healing that is hard-wired into your Core Soul from here on. This is not for requests requiring something to be healed, cleared, or removed from your energy, but for those *adding* a totally positive gift or benefit.

Be extremely careful of what you ask for, and with each request ask the Lords of Karma's permission to go forward.

1. Make your request, completing Lords of Karma processes I, II, and III and achieving a "yes" through the Outer Levels (Mind Grid, DNA, Karmic Contract, Core Soul level and beyond) and the Moment of Self.

2. Ask the Lords of Karma if your request may be *sealed unto the Light and unto protection forever.* If the answer is "yes," complete the process through all the levels and all the bodies, etc. If a "yes" is then granted, the process is complete. Say thank you.

3. If the answer is "no," it is either not needed or not appropriate for your request to be sealed unto the Light. There will usually be no clearing or release required. Complete the healing through all the levels and all the bodies, etc. If a "yes" is then granted, you are finished. Say thank you.

4. It takes approximately three weeks for a healing sealed unto the Light to be completed. You will feel gradual changes in your energy but few release symptoms. Once granted, know that it is done.

Sample healings: Offer your will (and/or hands) to the Goddess fully, completely, permanently, and forever. Dedicate yourself and your life to Goddess/God/The Light fully, completely, permanently, and forever.

Universal healings: Ask for complete Core Soul healing, and complete and permanent energy protection on all levels. Ask to forgive yourself and all others, ask for knowing that you deserve good in your life, and ask for positive self-love. Ask to heal, bring in, and integrate all alternate realities, and for reunion with your soul family.

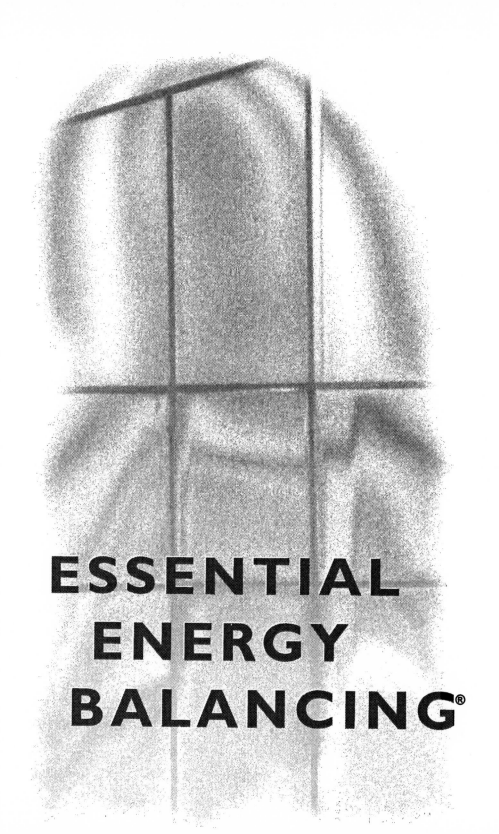

ESSENTIAL
ENERGY
BALANCING®

What Is Energy Balancing?

Now that you have learned to work with the Lords of Karma and are well on your way to healing fifty percent and more of the karma you came to this life with, it is time to begin Essential Energy Balancing®. This is a system of ten consecutive meditations to reprogram your Core Soul energy. The reprogramming is designed to heal all energy and vibrational damage in your Be-ing from the center of the Earth to your Moment of Self. It is also designed to reconnect you permanently with the Goddess Self that is your wholeness. We incarnate on Earth with only a fraction of our Be-ing, and Essential Energy Balancing® gives back to us a large part of who we really are.

The portion of our Spirit that incarnates in the Earth body is only an amount about the size of our thumb. In fact, we are vast Be-ings; we are angels and a part of Goddess. If our physical bodies represented all of us we would stand sixteen feet tall, and our auras would radiate a mile in all directions. We have been reduced by the disconnection of our DNA from thirty-eight strands to two. We have also been reduced by implants and negative interference, by the weight of karma that shadows our energy, and by the battering and damage our souls have received through hundreds of incarnations on Earth. Essential Energy Balancing® heals everything that has reduced us.

In our full intergalactic selves, human and animal DNA contains thirty-eight strands of coded genetic material. As part of the Earth experience, we were designed to have access to twelve of the strands. Our DNA contains and carries the encoded genetics of all of the life forms of the universe, what Barbara Marciniak in her book *Earth* calls the living library.

Embryologists who watch the evolution of mammals and birds from conception to birth are aware of the passage of life through several stages, from reptile and fish to animal and finally human form in the womb. Earth DNA now contains only two strands; we have been cut off from much of our heritage, and our development is limited by the loss.

Earth is a desirable planet by intergalactic standards. It is beautiful, optimal for life, has metals and other natural resources, and our DNA contains the living library. We were seeded here from twelve other planets, most of them in the Pleiadian Federation, and the Pleiadians are our foremothers. We did not evolve here, we were brought here. Other planets involved in Earth colonization include those in the Sirius and Orion systems. Since the time of Earth's inception, this planet has been the target of those who wish to control it (and us) for their own gain. Our enemies come primarily from the Orion system, though not all Orions wish us harm. The Pleiadians are the protectors of our freedom and free will, and of Earth's right to evolution and self-determination.

At some point in the war between the Pleiadians and Orion over the control or freedom of Earth, our twelve-strand DNA was unplugged to two strands. We lost most of our psychic abilities, as well as our communication with other dimensions and planets, and our physical contact with the rest of the inhabited universe. We lost the use of most of our brain function, the ninety-five percent of our potential that seems unaccessed in human physiology. We also lost the knowledge of who we are as Light Be-ings and members of an intergalactic community of planets and civilizations. While some psychics feel that this disconnection happened at least ten thousand years ago, I feel that it happened much more recently, within three thousand years. I believe that it coincided with the loss of the Goddess matriarchies through patriarchal takeover, and that it happened during or just after Old Testament times.

Regaining the use of our full Earth DNA, the twelve strands, is perhaps the greatest gift of all those being offered to us now.

It means an increase in our psychic abilities, channeling, access to spirit guidance, and other-dimensional communication and psychic travel. It also makes possible the healing of our karma, the raising of our energy vibration to the fifth dimension and beyond, reconnection to our outer octaves of energy bodies, reactivation of new chakras and chakra systems, and the return and rejoining with our Goddess Selves. Once we have completed the ascension process, we may be permitted the reconnection of the rest of our DNA, to bring the full complement to thirty-eight strands.

Further reduction of our energy and vibrational levels has come through interdimensional negative interference. The war for Earth has never been fair or ethical. Our enemies want to control us, both as individuals and the planet as a whole. We have been implanted again and again to reduce our abilities to function as free Be-ings, to control us, to interfere with who we are and with the possible healing of our reduced status. Virtually all of the healers and Lightworkers carry implants, which psychically appear in our energy as metal boxes or cylinders with wires attached. The boxes are often projectors or holograms that transmit fear—fear to keep us from becoming independent, to keep us from our life paths, and to hinder our work of healing people and the Earth. These implants reincarnate with us, and have been doing so for a few thousand years.

The interference occurs on both personal and planetary levels and is the source of *all* of Earth's violence and most of our suffering. Both violence and suffering are manifestations of fear. Interference is the source of conflict between nations and races, as we are fed the energies of fear and separation through the implants. Disruptive energy is also sent to Earth to create more fear, chaos, and disaster. While the war for the Earth has already been won on other dimensional levels, and we have won our planetary freedom, individuals must now be freed from implants and interference. This is also now possible, partly because of the DNA reconnection, and is addressed in a number of ways throughout the Energy Balancing process.

The weight of karma can now be cleared and our vibrational level can be raised to the point where karma no longer exists. Again the reconnection of our DNA and our willingness to work with the Lords of Karma to heal ourselves make this possible. Karma is primarily located in the Mind Grid, which is our individual part of the Earth Grid, the collective consciousness of the planet. As the karmic shadows are released from our Mind Grids, Light and healing enter where the shadows once kept them from entering. Light—in my definition of it—is information, vibration, Goddess, and healing energy. I once asked Brede what, if anything, exists beyond the Goddess and she replied, "Pure Light." The more of this Light that can safely enter our energy, the higher our vibration rises, the more the healing of karma and Core Soul damage can occur.

We are energy, living in a universe made of Light and vibration. That our bodies are solid is only temporary, only happening during Earth incarnation and incarnation on a few other planets. The reduction of our full Be-ing's Light necessary to fit us into an Earth body can also cause damage to our energy. Unhealed karma that moves higher and higher (or deeper and deeper) into our energy levels over many incarnations also causes damage to those levels. Many or most of us have been damaged by negative interference and energy attacks. Such damage can also happen between lifetimes and on outer levels that we may not be conscious of. As our Astral Twins are frequently fragmented by trauma, so can other of our Energy Selves. After hundreds of lifetimes on Earth, we need Core Soul healing, and the Energy Balancing system addresses this need.

I have mentioned Energy Selves several times, and it is now time to define them. As our full Light and energy is reduced so that we may enter the Earth body, our consciousness must also be reduced. Because of our limited two-strand DNA, we are not able to hold the full energy of our Be-ing safely. Most people are aware of having an Inner Child, a child consciousness within us. We in fact have a number of these consciousness levels, in ascending levels of awareness and wisdom. They may be the source in Goddess lore of the Maiden, Mother, and Crone, and also of the Seven Ages. These ages are the Infant Self, Inner Child, Maiden, Mother, Crone, and the Three-in-One Triple Goddess. Our Be-ing in physical body is the first of the Ages, since we represent all of them in turn as we grow and change throughout our lives.

The Energy Selves are located in our outer octave energy, in our Core Souls on ascending levels. Our Infant Self is also our Etheric Double and is located on the outer octave of our physical body energy. The astral body (outer octave of the emotional body) contains our Inner Child, who is also our Astral Twin. The Maiden is our Higher Self, located at the first spiritual body level. The causal body is the next layer of our spiritual bodies, containing two levels and two Energy Selves: the Essence Self, who is the Mother, at the galactic body, and the Goddess Self or Oversoul, the Crone, at the causal body.

We have had little contact with our Etheric Double because the Infant Self is pre-verbal and often asleep. Our Inner Child is becoming well known as a part of us who needs healing if we have been abused or incested. Many people know about the Higher Self; she is sometimes called our Whole Self or soul wisdom. Some people consider her to be Source energy, but she is only a part of it. She is the Maiden, and she has far greater wisdom than ours, with much more energy and initiative, but she is only the first level of soul wisdom. The Essence Self contains all of the learning from all of our incarnations on Earth; if the Maiden is innocence, the Essence Self is experience and the Mother. Her wisdom has been virtually untapped because we cannot access her without the twelve-strand DNA. She is all of who we have been and what we know.

The Goddess Self is our Oversoul and Goddess Within. Twenty-five to thirty-five Essence Selves are under the care of one Goddess Self and her Crone wisdom. At the conclusion of Essential Energy Balancing®, her energy will be joined fully with you again, and that wisdom made accessible. The clearing of fifty percent or more of your karma is required to do this. The

DIAGRAM 1

The Energy Selves

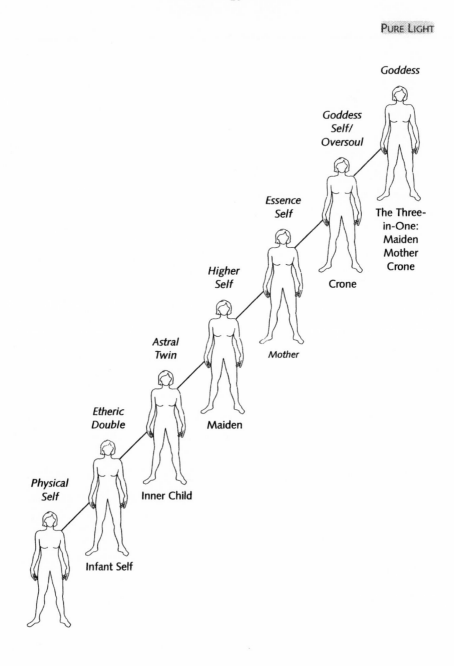

PURE LIGHT

Goddess

Goddess
Self/
Oversoul

Essence
Self

Goddess

Higher
Self

The Three-
in-One:
Maiden
Mother
Crone

Crone

Astral
Twin

Mother

Etheric
Double

Maiden

Physical
Self

Inner Child

Infant Self

Goddess Self's entrance and merging triggers ascension, the permanent evolutionary raising of your energy vibration to a level sufficient to contain the Light of your Goddess Self safely.

About twenty-five Oversouls/Goddess Selves are under the care of a Goddess, who is the Three-In-One or Oneself, the Maiden, Mother, and Crone. You will meet your Goddess, and about one in five hundred women (no men) will make permanent joining with her, as I have done with Brede. To do so, you must clear seventy-five percent or more of your Earth karma and go through a much more rigorous ascension process. The joining and ascension with Goddess or Goddess Self are the purpose of the Energy Balancing system.

Every culture and all the Earth religions have knowledge and stories about angels, their wonderful full wings and all the miracles they do to help people. As a Wiccan, I always assumed that angels were just another name for spirit guides, but this is not the case. When I first met my Higher Self, Essence Self, and Goddess Self I was amazed to see the visual images of women with wings. Our Energy Selves are angels and they are also us. The miracles come from our own higher Be-ings, from who we really are. Their wings are actually streams of Light energy radiating horizontally from the backs of their hearts (Moment of Self and Heart Complexes, to be exact). Not all angels are our Energy Selves, but our Energy Selves are all angels. In our fullness of Be-ing, we are a particular category of angels.

It is important to note here that our pets also have Energy Selves. When I called in the Energy Selves for my dogs Kali and Copper, I was delighted to see this, but I probably shouldn't have been so amazed. The dogs' Higher Selves came in as dog energy—dogs with wings! Their Essence Selves and Goddess Selves, however, were human and were my own Essence and Goddess Selves. They share a Goddess with me as well. When Brede joined with me in the ascension process, she also joined with them. Animals have karma to be healed just as humans do, and they have (and are) angels, too. Their energy systems are as complex as ours. They are not inferior to us. A pet that is close to you is probably a fragment of your own Core Soul and a member of your soul family.

Another energy component that is important in the Essential Energy Balancing® processes is the templates, the doorways or hatchways that connect the energy bodies to each other. Until these are aligned and cleared, the Energy Selves cannot move between bodies to enter your closer-to-physical conscious levels. Templates anchor into physical energy through the Crown chakra, but you will usually feel their activity in your Throat. The seven templates cleared and opened in the meditations are only one set of several—there are twenty-five templates and fifty-five energy bodies in all. Most of these are presently beyond our conscious reach.

The names given to the templates in this system come from Brede, but other healers working with them may have created different designations. When Brede first gave me the initial energy process, she told me clearly what to ask the Lords of Karma for. I had no idea at that time of what the templates are, nor did I understand most of the other energy components. I did not comprehend until much later what each meditation was for. The I-AM Template was discovered and named by five-year-old Josh Silverman, who informed me after we did a Process I Energy Balancing with him that we "forgot a temple, it's the I-AM Temple." After opening it for him, his mother Karen and I opened it for ourselves, and I began asking what it meant. This template opens the doorway for the Energy Selves to enter the closer-to-physical levels.

The first set of templates includes the Ka Template, between the physical and etheric bodies; the Etheric Template, between the Etheric and the emotional/astral levels; the Ketheric Template, between the emotional body and the mental body/Mind Grid; the Celestial Template, between the mental and spiritual bodies; and the I-AM Template, between the spiritual and galactic bodies. The outer templates in the series include the Galactic Templates (three of them) between the galactic and causal body, and the Causal Body Templates (three) between the causal body and the Goddess. These are the two causal body levels, the galactic body being the lower causal body, and the causal body itself being the higher level of the same body.

Another term used in the Energy Balancing meditations is the Silver Cord. This is a stream of Light that enters the body at the back of the heart. It is where the Energy Selves enter the closer-to-physical bodies, merging into the Heart Complex, a series of chakras accessed through all levels of the Heart. It is part of your Moment of Self. When your Heart Complex opens, your wings open, and you may feel them radiating. As the connection of your physical self to your Energy Selves, the Silver Cord is established at birth and its breaking or withdrawal normally means physical death. However, in the ascension process, after all the Energy Selves are merged and your Goddess Self (or Goddess) is fully integrated in your physical Be-ing, the Silver Cord phases out. It is no longer needed once the merging is complete.

The Grounding Cord is the Tube of Light that runs from the Moment of Self to the center of the Earth. At its outer levels it is called the Galactic Cord. This cord runs through all the templates and all the bodies and chakra systems, and enters the closer-to-physical bodies through the Transpersonal Point and Crown chakras. If you have difficulty functioning on the earth-plane, are spacey, clumsy, forgetful, or just can't seem to cope, it is because the Grounding Cord needs work. Properly reconnecting the cord to the center of the Earth makes all the difference in the world for comfort in living on this planet. A healed Grounding Cord makes astral travel and higher level psychic work safe and easy. It prevents Core Soul damage while traveling or being out of body.

It is important to know that there are chakra systems on each energy body (all fifty-five of them, though we won't work with that many). Most people know about the seven Kundalini chakras, but there are also thirteen chakras on the emotional body (Hara Line), and thirty-one on the mental body. Those on the mental body include ten finger tips and ten toe tips, both breasts, and chakras in the Crown complex, Third Eye complex, a pair of Light chakras at the temples, three chakras in the Throat complex, the Solar Plexus, and a chakra in the Root. The Hara Line emotional body chakras are the Transpersonal Point (Crown complex), Vision chakras (a pair) behind the eyes, Causal Body access chakra at the back of the head, Thymus chakra in the Heart Complex, Diaphragm chakra above the Solar Plexus, Hara chakra below the navel, Perineum chakra between the vagina opening and the anus, Movement chakras (a pair) at the back of the knees, Grounding chakras (a pair) in the feet, and the Earth chakra below the feet.

On the spiritual body and its two levels are two further sets of chakras. On the galactic lower level are seven chakras with access down the lower back. I have named these Will, Desire, Attainment, Action (a pair), and Propulsion (a pair). The first three are along the lower spine, Action is behind each knee, and Propulsion is at the heel of each foot. The causal body higher level series joins these down the upper back. I have named these chakras Sound (a pair), Reception/Information, Communication, Manifestation, Creation, and Implementation (a pair). Sound is located behind each ear, and Reception/Information is on the back of the head as an upper octave of the Causal Body chakra. Communication is where the neck and back meet. Manifestation is on the upper back. Creation is a part of the Moment of Self and Heart Complex and is located at the back of the Heart, and Implementation is a pair of chakras at each wrist. There is also the Spiritual, Galactic, and causal body Crown.

Much more data on energy structure is given later in this book, along with a complete set of diagrams. The above is basic information needed to understand what is happening in the Energy Balancing processes. If the material seems too complex, don't worry about it. You can achieve all you need to by going through the meditations themselves without worrying about the mechanics. I was given the structural how's and why's much later, usually some time after receiving each process. Brede channeled energy diagrams over a period of about a year, twenty-two of them in all. Much of the material was beyond my comprehension at the time. I received the meditations from her verbally and separately and did them without initially understanding the structures.

The series of ten meditation processes that follow are a unified series. They must be done *exactly in order* and with *exactly the wording given* in the text. This is very important. The meditations are incremental; each one depends on the one before it, and on your having completed the energy reprogramming of *all* the ones before it. If you attempt to take them out of order, the Lords of Karma will stop the process and not permit your going forward. The wording and order given for each process are also important. Each request is dependent upon your having completed the ones before it. Again, the Lords of Karma will usually stop the process if you attempt to take them out of order.

A woman who received the meditation scripts did the Chakra Complex Opening (Process VII), but did not open the chakras in the given order. For some reason, the Lords of Karma let her continue and finish the process. She called me several days later complaining of severe nausea that she felt was a direct result of the meditation. At first I thought that she was experiencing a clearing or detoxification reaction. Finally, however, she admitted to me that she had not done the process in the order it was written. I had her go to the Lords of Karma and ask what to do. They told her to repeat the meditation correctly, and when she did her nausea disappeared. That particular meditation done properly, by the way, is one of the most interesting of the series. Many people experience a sense of galaxies, lights, and universes with it, and no one else has told me of any difficulty or negative symptoms.

Though I give this series of ten processes in a weekend workshop intensive, I received them over a period of a year and a half, and did them for myself much more slowly. These processes and their actions on your energy are totally positive, but extremely intense. There is no need to do them quickly, as long as you do them incrementally (in order). Take whatever time you need to finish the series. You may repeat each meditation as many times as you wish before going to the next one, and may go back in the process to repeat those you have already completed. It may be best for most people to do only one new meditation per month, repeating the same one at least a few times before going on. Ask your Higher Self or the Lords of Karma what is best for you, and if you are ready to proceed.

Most of the meditations need to be done only once to achieve their needed effects, though these effects might not happen immediately. There is one exception: the second Essential Energy Balancing® process, which is a complete energy clearing. I have done this twice a day, morning and bedtime, for over a year now, and find it the most beneficial healing method I have yet discovered. Use it followed by an Essential Healing Circle before sleeping. It is best to do Process II before doing any new meditation (except Process V) for the first time. Once you have met your Energy Selves, you will also want to call them into your energy at least twice a day, and it is highly important to do so.

The sequence of meditation processes depends upon your ability to work with the Lords of Karma, but you will work with them here in a different way. Each meditation begins by asking to speak with the Lords of Karma and asking them to affect each step of the process. However, you will not receive "yes" and "no" responses to these requests. Instead, as soon as you ask for a process or step in each process, it will begin to occur. Only if you are not permitted to go ahead will the Lords of Karma intervene. In that case, you either receive a "no" in the way you are used to receiving it, or the process and energy movement will stop. If that happens, and it only rarely does, ask the Lords of Karma what is needed to go forward. Follow their directions and clear the "no" as you have before.

Though these processes are meditative, they are different from most of the meditations you are used to. They are best done lying down flat on your back in bed just before going to sleep. Make sure that your arms and legs are not crossed. You can prevent falling asleep simply by keeping your head and face turned forward in line with your body. Each mediation takes from fifteen minutes to half an hour. Relax and go to sleep at the completion of the process, but remain lying on your back. The energy reprogramming and sensations of the process will continue for at least another hour or two, often longer, but there is no need to stay awake unless you like to watch the fireworks, like me. If you wish, take the entire night to remain with the energy—you'll enjoy it.

Each process has a number of steps that are requests to the Lords of Karma. You will not be permitted to go to the next step until the first one is finished. If you insist on doing so, the Lords of Karma will call a halt and refuse to let you go on. For each step, you will know when it is time to continue by the sensations in your body. The energy moves through you from head to feet, and when it reaches your feet that step is done. When you feel the tingling in your feet, you may ask the Lords of Karma for the next step.

You may do these meditations by reading them step by step from this book, by making a separate list of the requests in order. You can buy my tapes from The Crossing Press or make a tape for yourself. Leave enough time between steps. You may find that you are going through the process as you read it to make the tape. If you need more time between steps than the taping allows, use the pause button. Using a battery-run Walkman-type cassette player with headphones is an easy way to do this; you can take it to bed with you. Make sure to leave yourself enough time between requests for the energy sensations to complete and to reach your feet. Some steps take longer than others for this to happen, from one to five minutes for each step, as long as fifteen or twenty minutes for Process V.

These ten meditations are interesting and pleasurable—they feel good. As they were given to me by Brede, I found each one different and all of them extremely exciting. You will see and feel things you have never experienced before, and discover a sense of bliss and joy that is totally new. As your Core Soul heals and twelve-strand DNA reactivates, you will discover aspects of yourself that you never knew were there. The entrance and merging of the Energy Selves brings a tremendous sense of love and of being loved. The further you go with these processes, the brighter and lighter your energy will become. You will feel your vibration increasing weekly. You will feel wonderful.

At the end of the ten meditations, most people will enter the clearing process that segues into ascension. This occurs more easily and frequently for women than for men. The beginning of ascension is an initiation, a rigorous period of death and rebirth and a journey to the Underworld. Its completion, however, makes the joy of the meditations and union with your Goddess Self permanent. It's worth the work and effort.

Let's begin with Process I.

Energy Balancing Process I

Do this meditation at bedtime just before you go to sleep. Lie on your back in bed, and do not cross your arms or legs. As you ask the Lords of Karma for each step, it will begin. If you receive a "no" at any time, ask what is needed to clear it and proceed when the "no" is cleared. Halts to the process happen infrequently, so expect to do the meditation from start to finish without discussion. These are processes you will feel in your body, and you may also receive visual images. Though the sensations may seem strange, relax and enjoy them, they are positive and safe.

Take the steps one at a time in order and complete each step before going on. You will know when a step is finished by the energy sensations moving to the bottoms of your feet. Each step takes about five minutes or less, but the DNA reconnection may take longer. As each Energy Self enters, you may wish to take time to talk with her before going on. Be careful not to fall asleep if you do this. If you fall asleep before completing all the steps, do the meditation again the next night and go further with it. The entire process takes about half an hour. It is very important to use the exact wording given for these meditations.

The requests for twelve-strand DNA and Core Soul healing need be asked for only once. They will be granted immediately, but the completion will not happen immediately. It takes about six months for full DNA reconnection and activation, and Core Soul healing may take longer if you have been heavily damaged. If you ask to heal, return, and integrate your soul fragments, the process can also take as long as three months, though you need ask for it only once. If you have already asked this of the Lords of Karma there is no need to repeat it now.

Not everyone receives the names of their Higher Self, Essence Self, and Goddess Self on the first try, though most will receive their Goddess' name more easily. She is someone you have always known and loved. If you cannot learn the name of one or more of your Energy Selves, you will do so later. Consider the contact enough for now; it is a major breakthrough. You may or may not receive visual images of your Energy Selves, but you will feel or see Light and energy and a definite presence. You will probably hear at least some of them speak to you.

When you have finished the meditation, remain relaxed and lie still, resting with the energy for some time. A couple of hours is optimal. You are welcome to fall asleep as soon as the process is finished and do your resting hours in that way. No matter how spacey you seem during and after the meditation, you will feel balanced and well in the morning.

PROCESS I:

The Opening Process

Important: Complete each step before going to the next (you will feel the energy reach your toes). Each step takes about five minutes.

1. Ask to speak with the Lords of Karma.
2. Ask them to align all your energy bodies and the connections between energy bodies.
3. Ask to clear, heal, align, open, activate, synchronize, fill with Light, repair, and reconnect your:
   a. Ka Template
   b. Etheric Template
   c. Ketheric Template
   d. Celestial Template
   e. I-AM Template

Do these one at a time in this order; finish each before asking for the next.

4. Ask to clear, heal, align, open, activate, synchronize, fill with Light, repair, and reconnect to the center of the Earth and beyond your Grounding Cord and its chakras, chakra complexes, channels, and connections on all levels.

5. Ask to clear, heal, align, open, activate, synchronize, fill with Light, repair, and reconnect your Silver Cord and chakras down the back on all levels.

6. Ask to clear, heal, align, open, activate, synchronize, fill with Light, repair, and reconnect your Heart Complex chakras and channels on all levels.

7. Ask to reconnect, heal, and activate your twelve-strand DNA.*

8. Ask for complete Core Soul healing on all levels.

9. (You can add optional other things here, like release all negative interference including psychic attacks, attachments, entities, elementals, and alien interference; clear your DNA of a dis-ease; heal, return, and integrate all soul fragments; heal and release all heart scars gently; open your psychic abilities; do a complete uncording, etc. You can ask to heal each aura body individually. Wait for the energy to move through with each request before asking for another item. Always ask for comfortable and easy integration of these healings.)

10. Ask your Higher Self to clear and activate your Ka Template, and to merge and anchor in with your Astral Twin, Etheric Double, and physical levels.

    a. ask your Higher Self her name
    b. ask her for a gift
    c. she will ask a gift of you
    d. invite her to remain connected with you permanently

11. Ask her to clear, heal, and fill your Hara Line chakras and channels.

12. Ask her to clear, heal, and fill your Kundalini Line chakras and channels.

13. Ask your Essence Self to clear and activate your Galactic chakras and templates on all levels, and to merge and anchor in with your Higher Self, Astral Twin, Etheric Double, and physical levels.

---

*Once you have completed Process X, you may ask the Lords of Karma to heal, reconnect, and activate the full complement of your DNA.

14. Ask your Essence Self for her name and she may have a message for you. Invite her to remain connected with you permanently.

15. Ask your Essence Self to clear, heal, and fill your mental body chakras and channels on all levels.

16. Ask your Goddess Self/Oversoul to clear and activate your causal body chakras and templates on all levels, and to merge and anchor in with your Essence Self, Higher Self, Astral Twin, Etheric Double, and physical levels.

17. Ask her name, talk with her. Invite her to remain connected with you permanently.

18. Ask your Goddess Self to clear, heal, and fill your spiritual body chakras and channels on all levels.

19. Invite your Goddess Self to remain connected with you permanently.

20. Ask your Goddess to merge and anchor in with you through all your levels, Energy Selves, and chakras, and through all the components of your Be-ing.

21. Ask your Goddess' name and talk with her. Invite her to remain connected with you permanently.

22. Ask for gentle integration of this healing, and that the processes and alignments just completed become permanent.

23. Come back to now, but remain lying still for the length of the experience. Rest with the energy for at least two hours if possible.

Energy Balancing Process II

The second Essential Energy Balancing® process is designed to be done repeatedly, daily, or even twice daily. Do this meditation in bed before sleep, or before doing any other new process (except Process V) for the first time. Do it lying on your back with your arms and legs straight. It takes about twenty minutes to do, but how well you feel after doing it makes it worth the effort. As you continue through the Energy Balancing series, your vibrational system begins to clear on all levels. Doing this process speeds the clearing and prevents jam-ups along the way. It clears and releases stagnant, stuck, or blocked energy in the channels, templates, bodies, and chakras. If at any time you feel uncomfortable because of detoxification symptoms, doing Process II will help to speed the energy release. It will also make it easier for you to connect with your Energy Selves and to deepen your contact with them.

Once you get the hang of this meditation, you may wonder whether you really need to do all the steps every time. Doing only the steps you need is fine as long as the steps are done in order. Do each step completely, however. To find out which steps you need on any given night, use a pendulum before you start and ask, "Do I need to align the energy bodies?" "Do I need to clear the templates?" If you do any of the templates, do all of them, and make sure to do them in order. Ask with each step whether you need that step or not. Once you have asked about the entire sequence, go back and do only the steps you need, skipping the ones you don't. This will speed the process if you don't want to do all of it. Be aware that what you need may be different each night, and that the more often you do this process the better you will feel.

The steps in Essential Energy Balancing® Process II are very similar to those in the opening process. With both processes you align the energy bodies, clear the templates, and clear the Grounding Cord, Silver Cord, and Heart Complex. With this process, however, you do not ask for DNA reconnection or Core Soul healing. Instead you ask to clear all of the energy bodies and their chakra systems that are within conscious reach. As in the first process, and all the processes, you will call in your Higher Self, Essence Self, Goddess Self, and Goddess at the end. The clearer your energy is, the deeper your connection with the Energy Selves can become. If the templates need clearing, your Energy Selves can't come in at all.

As your contact with your Energy Selves becomes clearer, begin to talk with them. Ask who they are, why they are there, and any questions you may have about the process or anything else. Your Higher Self especially becomes a good advisor for the complexities of daily life. If you do not have a verbal contact with these Selves, however, still know that the process is happening as it should.

A new energy component is introduced in this process. The astral sheath and etheric sheath are the auras surrounding these bodies. They are protective, like bags or amniotic sacs, and insulating for the bodies they surround. They are included here because they can be damaged or deflated and Process II helps to repair them.

Process II:

Daily Practice

Ask the Lords of Karma to do each of the following. It is important to allow each step to complete, which takes about five minutes, before going to the next. The step is finished when you feel the energy reach your feet.

1. Align all the energy bodies and the connections between energy bodies.

2. Ask to clear, heal, align, open, activate, synchronize, fill with Light, repair, and reconnect each of the following templates, one at a time.

   a. the Ka Template
   b. the Etheric Template
   c. the Ketheric Template
   d. the Celestial Template
   e. the I-AM Template
   f. the Galactic chakras and templates on all levels
   g. the Causal Body chakras and templates on all levels

3. Clear, heal, align, open, activate, synchronize, fill with Light, repair, and reconnect your Grounding Cord and its chakras, chakra complexes, channels, and connections on all levels.

4. Clear, heal, align, open, activate, synchronize, fill with Light, repair, and reconnect your Silver Cord and chakras down the back on all levels.

5. Clear, heal, align, open, activate, synchronize, fill with Light, repair, and reconnect your Heart Complex chakras and channels on all levels.

6. Clear, heal, align, open, activate, synchronize, fill with Light, repair, and reconnect the following energy bodies, one at a time:

   a. the spiritual, galactic, and causal bodies and the chakras, chakra complexes, channels, and connections on those levels.
   b. the mental body and Mind Grid and the chakras, chakra complexes, channels, and connections on those levels.
   c. the emotional and astral bodies, Astral Twin, astral sheath, and the chakras, chakra complexes, channels, and connections on those levels.
   d. the physical and etheric bodies, Etheric Double, etheric sheath, and the chakras, chakra complexes, channels, and connections on those levels.

Individual chakras on all levels:

    a. The Spiritual, Galactic, and Causal body crown

    b. Causal body chakras—Sound, Reception/Information, Communication, Manifestation, Creation, Implementation

    c. Galactic chakras—Will, Desire, Attainment, Action, Propulsion

    d. Mental body chakras—Crown, Third Eye, Light chakras, three Throat chakras (at the lips, top of throat, and lower throat), Solar Plexus, Root, breast tips, finger tips, toe tips

    e. Emotional body (Hara) chakras—Transpersonal Point, Vision chakras, Causal Body chakra, Thymus chakra, Diaphragm chakra, Hara chakra, Perineum chakra, Movement chakras, Grounding chakras, Earth chakra

    f. Etheric body (Kundalini) chakras—Crown, Third Eye, Throat, Heart, Solar Plexus, Belly, Root

7. Ask your Higher Self to clear and activate the Ka Template, and to merge and anchor in with your Astral Twin, Etheric Double, and physical level fully, completely, and permanently.

8. Ask your Higher Self to clear, heal, and fill your chakras and channels on all levels.

9. Ask your Essence Self to clear and activate the Galactic chakras and templates, and to merge and anchor in with your Higher Self, Astral Twin, Etheric Double, and physical level fully, completely, and permanently.

10. Ask your Essence Self to clear, heal, and fill your chakras and channels on all levels.

11. Ask your Goddess Self to clear and activate the Causal body chakras and templates, and to merge and anchor in with your Essence Self, Higher Self, Astral Twin, Etheric Double, and physical level fully, completely, and permanently.

12. Ask your Goddess Self to clear, heal, and fill your chakras and channels on all levels.

13. Ask your Goddess to merge and anchor in with all your levels, Energy Selves, chakras, and all the components of your Be-ing fully, completely, and permanently.

14. Thank the Lords of Karma and your Energy Selves, and come back to now when ready. It is best to do this in bed and go to sleep for the night to finish it. Once you reach Process V, you may wish to start an Essential Healing Circle before finishing.

Energy Balancing Process III

This meditation requires more direct working with the Lords of Karma. After each of the clearing steps, the Lords of Karma are asked to take the healing through the Outer Levels (Mind Grid, DNA, Karmic Contract, Core Soul level and beyond), and from below the center of the Earth to beyond the Moment of Self. You may receive a "yes" or "no" to these requests. Do not ask for sealing unto the Light and unto protection yet, but you may do so once you have done the process several times. The Lords of Karma will tell you when you may do this. Ask them from time to time whether you are ready for it, but do not proceed until they tell you to. The usual Lords of Karma finish (all the levels and all the bodies, etc.) is not needed for this process.

The format for this meditation is different from others in the Essential Energy Balancing® series. After asking to align the energy bodies, start steps two through nine by asking the Lords of Karma to clear, heal, align, open, activate, synchronize, fill with Light, repair, and reconnect each item. When the energy reaches your feet, ask for the healing through the four Outer Levels, and then through the Moment of Self for each step, including the first. If you receive a "no" at any time, stop and clear it. After requesting and being granted the clearing through the Moment of Self for each component, ask for the healing fully, completely, permanently, and forever for each.

In this process, ask to clear, heal, align, etc., all of the templates at once, instead of one at a time. Ask to clear, heal, align, etc. each energy body and its outer octave one at a time. The spiritual, galactic, and causal bodies are included in one request.

The mental body and Mind Grid are a separate request. Ask for the emotional body, astral body, and Astral Twin at once, and for the physical body, etheric body, and Etheric Double at once. This time the various chakras on each level are not asked for individually, but one request asks for all of them together. All of the Energy Selves are cleared, healed, aligned, etc. at once, as well. Once the process is finished, you may call in your Energy Selves if you wish to.

The new energy component for this process is the energy transformers. In our Be-ings' electrical systems, there are many controls for stepping down our full energy so that it may be housed in the physical body. These transformers, or more accurately transforming processes, can occasionally need clearing and sometimes need to be repaired. Various types of Core Soul damage can cause these transformers to malfunction. They are healed by the simple request to do so, and to do so in a permanent way.

This process moves very quickly once you get the hang of it, and only takes a few minutes to do. Do not be in a hurry to seal the requests unto the Light—give time for the full healing at each level to take place. You have asked to make the clearing, healing, aligning, etc. permanent at each level, and this takes some time to bring into effect and completion. Though Process III seems similar to the previous meditations, it is not. The requests are becoming incremental now—you are asking for the first time to make the healings permanent. This is a more important step than it appears to be.

As with the other Energy Balancing meditations, this one is best done lying in bed, the last thing at night before sleep. Remember to lie on your back, with arms and legs resting straight and uncrossed. Each step is finished when you feel the energy reach your feet. The steps must be done in order and using the precise wording given in the text. These first three meditations are primarily designed for clearing your energy. The next process starts anchoring in the Energy Selves and bringing them toward merging and ascension.

PROCESS III:

Core Soul Healing

A. *To Start Each:* Ask the Lords of Karma to clear, heal, align, open, activate, synchronize, fill with Light, repair, and reconnect items 2 through 9. (For item 1, ask only to align, and for item 10, ask as written.)

B. *After Each:* Ask for the healing through the Outer Levels (Mind Grid, DNA, Karmic Contract, Core Soul level and beyond) and from below the center of the Earth to beyond your Moment of Self. Ask for a response with each; if any request is "no" ask how to clear it and do so. (All the levels and all the bodies, etc. is not needed with this process. Do not ask for sealing unto the Light and unto protection yet.)

C. *To End Each:* Ask for the healing fully, completely, permanently, and forever with each item.

1. Align all the energy bodies and connections between energy bodies.

2. All the templates at once.

3. Your Grounding Cord and its chakras, chakra complexes, channels, and connections on all levels.

4. The Silver Cord and chakras down the back on all levels.

5. Your Heart Complex chakras and channels on all levels.

6. Each energy body and its chakras and channels on all levels:
   - a. spiritual, galactic, and causal bodies
   - b. mental body and Mind Grid
   - c. emotional body, astral body, and Astral Twin
   - d. physical body, etheric body, and Etheric Double

7. All the chakras, chakra complexes, channels, and connections on all levels.

8. All the Energy Selves, soul components, and the connections between them (at once).

9. All energy transformers.

10. Full protection and *gentle* energy purification on all levels.

11. Ask that all the healings happen gently and comfortably, and integrate fully on all levels.

Thank the Lords of Karma, and come back when you are ready. Give yourself at least half an hour to rest with the energy. If doing this in bed at night, you may go to sleep as soon as the process is finished.

After doing the process many times: Ask the Lords of Karma if you may "seal these healings unto the Light and unto protection forever." When they agree to your readiness, ask for it at the end of each item.

Energy Balancing Process IV

This is the first ascension process, as in it you will ask your Energy Selves, Goddess, and the Light Beyond the Goddess to anchor into your energy permanently. Until now, the Energy Selves have come in when invited but they have not stayed. Now they are tied, but not yet fully joined, into your closer-to-physical levels and will remain connected. The clearing and repairing steps of the previous meditations make this tying in possible, and it is a milestone in the Energy Balancing system. It is extremely important to use the *exact wording* given for these requests; this is so for all of the Essential Energy Balancing® meditations, but particularly for the three ascension processes and the Light Body Activation at the end. I cannot emphasize the importance of this enough.

As with the other meditations, this one is best done lying on your back with arms and legs kept straight. Bedtime is the best time to do this, as most energy reprogramming on nonphysical levels happens during sleep, and the requests you make are put into effect then. This is why some people feel a need to sleep more while working with the Essential Energy Balancing® and ascension processes; the Lords of Karma, your Energy Selves, and your Goddess do the mechanics of your healing at this time. If you feel tired, understand that the amount of healing you are doing on other levels is intense, and that healing is its own form of heavy work. You may wish to repeat Process II before beginning this meditation, particularly before doing it for the first time.

The Light beyond the Goddess is a new energy structure term for Process IV. When discovering the Energy Selves, I found each one in turn by asking Brede what came after the ones I had already met. When we reached the Goddess level where she is, and I asked her what came next, her reply was "Pure Light." Beyond the Goddess is the Light beyond the Goddess, or the Radiance of the Light. This is the place where souls are formed and what they are formed from. As a soul emerges from the Light beyond the Goddess, it differentiates from the Source. This is the Moment of Self. When we become ourselves instead of a part of the One, we feel separation for the first time. All of our lives and lifetimes are a quest to return to that Oneness, to the Light Beyond the Goddess, and to heal our separation from it. This is the root cause of all abandonment, loneliness, isolation, and separation on Earth. It is positive to go to the Lords of Karma and ask to heal your separation from the Source; most people will find trauma or sadness there. It is also positive to ask them to heal your Moment of Self.

This is a Lords of Karma process similar to the last one, and you may receive "yes" and "no" responses from them. If you receive a "no" at any time, stop and clear it before going further. By this time in the energy series, it is rare to be refused, but it can happen. Clearing a "no" at this level can be highly revealing, and these karmic healings will be life-changing.

In this meditation, you will ask the Lords of Karma to anchor each of the Energy Selves, one at a time in order from the Goddess to the Etheric Double, into you fully, completely, and permanently so she may work through you. Use this wording exactly. Ask for the anchoring of each through the Outer Levels (Mind Grid, DNA, Karmic Contact, Core Soul level and beyond), from below the center of the Earth to beyond your Moment of Self, and seal the healing unto the Light and unto protection forever. For six Energy Selves, you will make this request to the Lords of Karma six times. All the levels and all the bodies, etc. is not needed.

Do the next requests (2 through 4) in the same manner to ask for complete healing of all connecting channels between the Energy Selves, then for complete synchronization of the Energy

Selves and their channels. Disturbance or damage in the channels or lack of vibrational synchronization can prevent the Energy Selves from fully entering your closer-to-physical energy. By asking for permanent healing of the channels and permanent synchronization, you figuratively pave the highway for them to travel to you on. Next, ask to anchor in the Light beyond the Goddess through all your Energy Selves, as fully as you can comfortably receive this Light, and ask to seal it unto the Light and unto protection forever. It is not necessary, though you may do it if you wish, to go through the Outer Levels and whole Lords of Karma process for these requests.

You will next ask to anchor in each Energy Self in turn as above, fully, completely, and permanently through all the chakras and channels at all the levels. This is another Lords of Karma process. Go through the Outer Levels, Moment of Self, and Sealing unto the Light and unto protection for each, as well as through all the levels and all the bodies, etc. Do the same with the Light beyond the Goddess, also asking to expand your energy to be able to receive as much of this Light as possible. At the end of the sequence, ask for easy integration of these healings; they are intensive changes to your energy.

The sensations you will experience doing this process are extremely joyful. There is great bliss in bringing the Energy Selves and the Goddess home. Remain quiet for at least an hour (more if possible) after completing the meditation, and it is better yet to sleep overnight while the healing continues and completes.

PROCESS IV:

The First Ascension Process

1. Ask the Lords of Karma to anchor each of the Energy Selves (one at a time below) into you fully, completely, and permanently so she may work through you. When this is granted, go to the Outer Lords of Karma levels with each: Mind Grid level, DNA level, Karmic Contract level, and Core Soul Level and beyond. Next, ask for the healing from below the center of the Earth to beyond your Moment of Self. Finally, ask that each Energy Self's anchoring be

sealed unto the Light and unto protection forever. (All the levels and all the bodies, etc. is not needed with this process.)

    a. Goddess

    b. Goddess Self

    c. Essence Self

    d. Higher Self

    e. Astral Twin (ask to heal and anchor)

    f. Etheric Double (ask to heal and anchor)

2. Ask for complete healing of all connecting channels between the Energy Selves.

3. Ask for complete synchronization of all the Energy Selves and their channels.

4. Ask to anchor in the Light beyond the Goddess through all of your Energy Selves as fully as is optimal for you, permanently and completely, and seal it unto the Light and unto protection, forever.

5. Starting with the Goddess and asking separately for each Energy Self: ask the Lords of Karma to anchor in each Energy Self fully, completely, and permanently through all the chakras and channels at all the levels. Ask that the healing be carried through the Outer Levels (Mind Grid, DNA, Karmic Contract, Core Soul level and beyond), and through your Moment of Self. Ask that each be sealed unto the Light and unto protection forever, and finish with all the levels and all the bodies, etc. Do this with each Energy Self one at a time as above. You may wish to do this in a different energy session.

6. Ask to anchor in the Light beyond the Goddess through all of your chakras and channels at all the levels, as fully, completely, and permanently as is optimal for you. Ask also to expand your energy to be able to accept as much Light as possible. Ask for the healing through the outer karmic levels, through your Moment of Self, and seal it unto the Light and unto protection forever. Ask for the healing through all the levels and all the bodies, etc.

7. Ask the Lords of Karma for gentle and easy integration of these healings on all levels.

8. Thank the Lords of Karma and your Energy Selves. Rest with the energy for at least an hour before getting up, or do the meditation at bedtime and go to sleep at the end.

Energy Balancing Process V
and Essential Healing Circle

Everyone looks for a shortcut. Sometimes you just don't want to spend half an hour or an hour clearing your energy so you can start another half-hour process. Sometimes the path to enlightenment just seems too darn hard and you'd rather go to sleep. Sometimes it's just too late at night.

Leave it to Western culture to look for the quick fix; there must be one here somewhere and this is it. It's something to use once in a while, but the quick fix is not for every day. To do this shortcut you must have the Lords of Karma's permission. If they grant it, go ahead. If your energy is relatively clear, they will likely say "yes," but otherwise you will be required to go through the whole routine of Process II. Either way, if you do full energy clearing often, you will feel wonderful.

The steps in this process require you to be lying down and completely quiet in body and mind. Each step takes longer than the usual Energy Balancing release, as you are clearing multiple energy components at one time. The first step may take as long as twenty minutes. You will feel energy move from head to feet in waves. The first time it reaches your feet may not be the finish, as another wave of energy comes close behind. When *all* the energy movements reach your feet and everything stops, the step is done. Do each step of the process in this way.

The Emergency Clearing moves through all of your energy components in four steps, but you or the Lords of Karma can stop it at any point. If the Lords of Karma stop it, it is because the full process is needed; there is too much blockage or congestion in your vibration at this time for shortcuts. You may also stop at any step in the process if you do not wish to do them all. The steps must be done in order, however, and to do each step you must complete all the steps previous to it.

At the finish of step four, you may end the session or enter an Essential Healing Circle for whatever type of healing you may designate. For the first several times, at least five, you must do the full Essential Healing Circle process given below. After five times of calling in the same list of Light Be-ings, you may simply ask to enter an Essential Healing Circle for your chosen process. Once you have done the Emergency Clearing or Process II and asked to enter the Healing Circle, you may go to sleep and the healing will continue. This combination makes for a wonderfully restful night and accomplishes significant healing of your energy.

The Essential Healing Circle is a method of creating your own discarnate healing team. Similar processes exist that name the Be-ings to ask into such teams, but this is the only one that you design for yourself. It is suggested that you use the format given below, but it is not required. The basic Be-ings that you will wish to invite to make up your team include the Healing Angels of the Light; your Goddess, Nada, and the Lords of Karma; your Higher Self, Essence Self, and Goddess Self. These are numbers one to three in the process. Everyone else is subject to your own affinities and wishes. You may invite any deities, spirit guides, angels, or healers you need or wish to have with you. You can designate angels or healers by what they do if you don't know their names—the Angel of Healing Relationships, for example, or the Angel of Protection. I encourage you to invite the Angels of Grace and of Mercy into your Healing Circle.

Once you decide who your team is to consist of, try the Essential Healing Circle. You may make additions or adjustments as you go along. When your team settles into a full complement of healers for every session, and you use that team in Essential Healing Circles five times, they become your permanent Healing

Circle team. From that point on, you only need to ask for an Essential Healing Circle, and they will come and work on you.

You may designate an Essential Healing Circle for a specific purpose, or for overall healing. The purpose can change every time you use the Circle. The examples listed here will get you started, but you can designate a Circle for any positive use or reason. If you don't know which Healing Circle to try, just ask for Healing on All Levels, or ask for something that you feel you need. You can use these Circles to help with decision making, clearing detoxification symptoms, getting a good night's sleep, or energy repair of any type. You may use it to meet with any of your Energy Selves or your Goddess, or to be filled with the Light beyond the Goddess (try it, it's lovely). If you have been doing a great deal of Lords of Karma or Essential Energy Balancing® work, an Essential Healing Circle for Integration and Rebalancing can help tremendously with both your comfort and your progress.

Note that when asking for angels, intergalactic healers, and others, I specify that they be "of the Light." While I have never met any other type of angel than those of positive intent, some cultures believe that these exist, and I want to make perfectly sure that only Light Be-ings enter my energy. This is also true for intergalactic Be-ings; there are both positive and negative ones, and only the positive are wanted. If you have any doubt of the intentions of an energy entering your presence, ask it immediately if it comes from the Light or from the Goddess. Universal Law requires a true answer. If the energy is negative, it will respond to your request either by identifying itself in some way as undesirable, or by leaving. Any negative energy must leave if you tell it to do so. If it doesn't, call for the Lords of Karma, your Guardian Angels of the Light, or the Angels of Blue Lightning to remove it.

As with other processes, do this one lying on your back with arms and legs uncrossed.

Process V:

Emergency Clearing

This is an emergency process and not for everyday use. The requests may or may not be granted and the process may be stopped at any point. If the first request is granted, remain lying down and completely quiet in body and mind until it is finished before requesting the next step. You may stop at any step or do all of the sections, but you must do them in order, and to do each step you must complete all steps previous to it.

1. Ask the Lords of Karma for complete Energy Balancing on all levels.

2. Ask the Lords of Karma to clear and activate all the templates and merge and anchor in your Higher Self, Essence Self, and Goddess Self through your Astral Twin, Etheric Double, and physical levels, fully, completely, and permanently. (This is done all at once.)

3. Ask your Higher Self, Essence Self, and Goddess Self to clear, heal, and fill all your chakras and channels on all levels.

4. Invite your Goddess to merge and anchor in with you through all the levels and components of your Be-ing.

5. Ask to enter an Essential Healing Circle for the process of your choice. See the next section. You must have done the full Essential Healing process at least five times before requesting it in short form.

Remain quiet until all processes are completed. This is best done in bed before the night's sleep.

Essential Healing Circle

Do this in bed before sleep, after completing a full Energy Balancing Process II or V, and bringing in your Higher Self, Essence Self, Goddess Self, and Goddess. The Be-ings invoked are subject to your preferences and choice—feel free to delete or add to the ones listed below. Invite them in, in order, ask for the type of healing or Healing Circle needed, and then go to sleep. Expect to remain quiet for up to three hours. After establishing the process and your personal series of Be-ings to invoke, and using the process at least five times, you may simply ask to open an Essential Healing Circle for the process of your choice.

To begin, after bringing in your Energy Selves, state: *"I ask also to join me..."*

1. The Healing Angels of the Light
2. Your Goddess *(name)*, Nada, and The Lords of Karma
3. Your Higher Self, Essence Self, and Goddess Self
4. The Radiance of the Light beyond the Goddess
5. Intergalactic Healers of the Light
6. The Angel of Grace and Angel of Mercy
7. Any other angels for your need—by name or what you need done, i.e., the Angel of Soul Retrieval, Angel of Love, Angel of Protection, Raphael, Ariel, Michael, etc.
8. Your guardian angels, guides, and healers of the Light

Next, ask for the type of healing needed. Ask to enter an Essential Healing Circle for *(your choice)*. Some possible examples are:

> Healing on all levels
>
> DNA repair and reconnection
>
> Energy clearing and purification
>
> Cellular repatterning
>
> Recovery and rejuvenation
>
> Healing sleep
>
> Abundance and manifesting
>
> Core Soul healing and repair
>
> Healing and repair of a specific energy component or energy body
>
> Uncording and unhooking on all levels
>
> Clearing negative interference
>
> Soul retrieval
>
> Integration and rebalancing
>
> Spiritual growth and evolution
>
> Ascension preparation
>
> Holy union and merging (do as a couple)
>
> Karmic healing and release

Healing a specific condition

Hormonal rebalancing

Rebalancing physical chemistry or brain chemistry

Meeting with your Higher Self

Meeting with your Essence Self

Meeting with your Goddess Self

Meeting with your Goddess

Meeting with the Light Beyond the Goddess

Divine or angelic love and healing

Energy Balancing Process VI

This is the next step on the ascension path, and it is a major one. In Process IV, you asked to anchor each of your Energy Selves into your closer-to-physical levels. This time, you ask for deeper connection, merging, and the beginning of fusion. You will first ask to *merge and fuse* your Etheric Double and Astral Twin with your physical levels. This raises your physical level and the levels of the two lower Energy Selves (whom you have not met as separate Be-ings), then *merges* your Higher Self into and through them. Your physical levels are raised to join with your Infant Self, and both are raised to join with your Inner Child. The Etheric Double and Astral Twin are absorbed into the consciousness of the Maiden. The Infant and Child have begun to grow up, and the Maiden/Higher Self moves through your increased energy. Though she is not yet fused into you, she still goes in and out, her presence grows considerably. *DO NOT FUSE your Higher Self and Astral Twin* as yet, only merge them. This is very important.

Next, your Higher Self, Essence Self, and Goddess Self are *merged and fused* fully, completely, and permanently. They become one Be-ing, that of your Goddess Self. Your connections with Goddess are then *merged and fused* with your Goddess Self, Essence Self, and Higher Self, and with your Astral Twin, Etheric Double, and physical levels. The Goddess works through all your Energy Selves and levels. The Light beyond the Goddess is next *merged only* through all the levels and components of your Be-ing. These steps begin the creation of your Light Body.

Eventually, all the Energy Selves are fused into your Goddess

Self, but now is not the time. It is important to not rush the process and to do this meditation exactly as it's written. You are not ready for full fusion as yet, but will be soon. To do so now would greatly overload your energy system, and Core Soul damage may result. Your vibrational levels are not healed or raised high enough yet. Please take these warnings seriously.

As in other processes, this one is best done lying flat in bed just before sleep. Doing a full energy clearing (Process II) first is highly beneficial. The sensations and colors that go with this healing are too wonderful to miss or cut short; without moving, go to sleep upon finishing the meditation and spend the night enjoying them. Though you may feel very spacey while they are happening, you will be grounded and well in the morning, and easily able to handle daily life.

This is a Lords of Karma process, but you will rarely be stopped with a "no" to these requests. If you are stopped, however, you have become an expert by now at clearing refusals. If the Lords of Karma tell you that you are not ready to do this process, you must obey them and wait. Ask what you need in order to be ready and follow their instructions. Continue doing energy clearing with Process II and Essential Healing Circles, as well as the previous Essential Energy Balancing® meditations. Do not go forward to new work until you are able to finish this process. Wait a week or so, then ask the Lords of Karma again if you may do the meditation. The process usually needs to be done only once, but you may repeat it if you wish.

PROCESS VI:

The Second Ascension Process

This may be done only after work with the previous processes, and only after completing Energy Balancing Process IV.

Do not ask to *fuse* your Astral Twin and Higher Self, only to *merge* them. Before beginning, do a full energy clearing (Process II) and bring in all of your Energy Selves. If the Lords of Karma refuse your request for this process, do not continue.

1. Ask the Lords of Karma to *merge and fuse* your Astral Twin, Etheric Double, and physical levels fully, completely, and permanently. Ask for the healing through the Outer Levels (Mind Grid, DNA, Karmic Contract, Core Soul level and beyond). Ask for the healing from below the center of the Earth to beyond your Moment of Self, and that the healing be sealed unto the Light and unto protection forever. Ask for all the levels and all the bodies, etc.

2. Ask the Lords of Karma to *merge only* your Higher Self with your Astral Twin, Etheric Double, and physical levels fully, completely, and permanently. *DO NOT FUSE.* Ask for the healing through the Outer Levels, through your Moment of Self, and sealed unto the Light and protection forever. Ask for all the levels and all the bodies, etc.

3. Ask the Lords of Karma to *merge only* your Higher Self, Essence Self, and Goddess Self fully, completely, and permanently. Ask for the healing through the Outer Levels, through your Moment of Self, and sealed unto the Light and unto protection forever. Ask for all the levels and all the bodies, etc.

4. Ask the Lords of Karma to *merge and fuse* your connections with Goddess with your Goddess Self, Essence Self, and Higher Self. Ask to *merge and fuse* your connections with Goddess with your Astral Twin, Etheric Double, and physical levels fully, completely, and permanently. Ask for the healing through the Outer Levels, through your Moment of Self, and sealed unto the Light and unto protection forever. Ask for all the levels and all the bodies, etc.

5. Ask the Lords of Karma to *merge* (only) the Light beyond the Goddess through all the levels and components of your Be-ing fully, completely, and permanently. Ask for the healing through the Outer Levels, through your Moment of Self, and sealed unto the Light and unto protection forever. Ask for all the levels and all the bodies, etc.

Take the time that you need to rest and experience the healing. At least two hours is recommended. This meditation is best done in bed at night, just before sleep.

Energy Balancing Process VII

That we are complicated Be-ings is obvious by now to anyone who has come through Essential Energy Balancing® so far. Our physical existence is so very small, but we are so very vast. We are truly angels and Goddesses, and a part of the Radiance of the Light, but we have so little idea of this or of what it means. Some of this unknowing is the necessity of Earth incarnation. To enter an Earth body, we must leave behind the greatest part of ourselves. Our vastness must reduce to the very little bit of energy our two-strand DNA and Earth bodies can allow us to contain. We lose our Selves and our knowledge of our Selves, and perhaps only this loss makes incarnation bearable. Yet we are also terrified to die and to leave the limitations of Earth behind. Those who have worked with the Lords of Karma and met their Energy Selves also lose the fear of death.

I did a Lords of Karma telephone healing with a woman who was having difficulty in expressing her personal truths. I had her go to the Lords of Karma to heal and open her Throat chakra, and she thought I said Throat Complex. She reported seeing a spiraling galaxy of energy that went up and up, and lights and fireworks to match. "There's a whole lot more than one chakra out there," she said. "How many are there?" I asked her, fascinated by now. Said the woman, "Someone just told me seventy-two." Then I asked the Lords of Karma to heal and open my own Throat Complex, and was amazed by the light show, as well. "Wow," I said, "and there are six more chakras on this level alone (the Kundalini Line) to try!"

That night, I asked to heal, open, and activate all the seventy-two chakras on all levels of the entire Kundalini Line, chakra by chakra, starting at the Crown. I suspected that some of the complexes also contain more than seventy-two; the Heart has a hundred and eight. The lights and colors upon opening these chakra complexes were wonderful, and since the Lords of Karma applauded when I made the request, I knew I was on to something. Brede suggested taking the process through all of the Lords of Karma levels and this meditation was born. Do it lying in bed and watch a show that makes the Fourth of July look austere.

A chakra complex is a series of chakras, that while existing on many energy body levels, have outlet through the Kundalini (etheric body) Line. The energy of many, but not all, of our bodies reaches our physical makeup in this way. After understanding that, I had to ask just how many bodies there really are. Then how many templates. And whether there were more Energy Selves than I knew of. I was amazed to be told that there are twenty-five templates that we need to know about (and probably more that we don't). There are fifty-five energy bodies, each with its own system of chakras, most of which are beyond our present knowing and access. There were no new Energy Selves to discover, but four Be-ings who called themselves Guardians appeared at a very far away level. They are the Guardians of the Four Directions that Wiccans know, but I was surprised to find them to be part of our personal energy.

Next, I had to ask that if we have so many chakras entering the Kundalini system, can those chakra complexes carry the negative cords and hooks that the etheric chakras do? I was told "yes," and when I asked to clear mine, was surprised at how far out such attachments exist. I have worked for several years at clearing cords and hooks from my energy, but still found more when I asked to clear them from the chakra complexes. Another part of this process began.

A woman who went through the Energy Balancing meditations did this series of requests, but took the chakra complexes out of order. After experiencing nausea for several days, she called me for help. When we figured out that the problem was taking the steps out of order, I asked her to go to the Lords of Karma to heal it. They told her to repeat the meditation, doing it correctly, and when she did her nausea abated. A word to the wise should be sufficient. As in all of these processes, you must do them as given, in order, using the exact wording. Done correctly, this meditation is one of the most pleasurable and memorable ones in Essential Energy Balancing®.

PROCESS VII:

Opening the Chakra Complexes

1. Ask the Lords of Karma to heal, open, and activate the seventy-two-plus chakras on all levels of the following chakra complexes. Do them one at time. With each, go to the Outer Levels (Mind Grid, DNA, Karmic Contract, Core Soul level and beyond), from below the center of the Earth to beyond the Moment of Self, and ask that the healing be sealed unto the Light and unto protection forever. (All the levels and all the bodies, etc. is not needed.)

> Crown Complex
> Third Eye Complex
> Throat Complex
> Heart Complex
> Solar Plexus Complex
> Belly Complex
> Root Complex

2. Ask the Lords of Karma to remove very gently all negative cords and hooks from all seventy-two-plus chakras on all levels and all chakra complexes. Go to the Outer Levels (Mind Grid, DNA, Karmic Contract, Core Soul level and beyond), and through the Moment of Self. Do not seal this request unto the Light. (All the levels and all the bodies, etc. is not needed.)

3. Ask the Lords of Karma to heal, open, and activate each of the following. Go to the Outer Levels, the Moment of Self, and seal each healing unto the Light and unto protection forever. (All the levels and all the bodies, etc. is not needed.)

> the 25 templates at all levels
> the 55 energy bodies at all levels

the 7 energy selves and 4 guardians

the energy connections at all levels

all the levels and components of your Be-ing

4. Thank the Lords of Karma and ask that these healings integrate comfortably and gently on all levels. Give yourself time to rest and experience the process; at least two hours is needed.

Energy Balancing Process VIII

This process consists of only three requests to the Lords of Karma, but the power of the three steps is immense. We are at the point of full fusion and complete merging of the Energy Selves and creation of the ascended body of Light, your fifth-dimensional self. By now, you have become very familiar with your Energy Selves and Goddess. You have experienced the Light, and the feeling of being filled with the Radiance of the Light beyond the Goddess. As the fusion continues, your Higher Self absorbs your combined Etheric Double and Astral Twin, and in turn is absorbed into your Essence Self. Next, the combined Selves—Etheric Double, Astral Twin, Higher Self, and Essence Self—are merged, fused, and absorbed into your Goddess Self/Oversoul.

In Energy Balancing Process VI, your Higher Self was fused with your Essence Self and Goddess Self. She was only merged, however, with your fused physical level, Etheric Double, and Astral Twin. Now the three outer Selves are joined with the three inner ones, and all the Selves made one. Until now, you have had primary conversation and contact with your Higher Self, but suddenly when you ask for her your Essence Self is there. Eventually only your Goddess Self appears, a single voice or presence instead of three. Your Goddess remains separate and Herself, but She and the Light beyond the Goddess are fused within you permanently. The completion of these changes takes about three weeks.

These mergings and joining together are highly positive. They are a process similar to growing up, the growing up and maturing of the vibration of your soul. Your Goddess Self is your

Oversoul and an angel, and she is Crone wisdom. Though she may not appear to you as old, she is ancient. The last of the Energy Selves to come into focus for you as a separate Be-ing, your Goddess Self has her own personality and opinions. You may ask her questions about anything from who she is and who you are in relation to her, to questions about your daily life. If you are unable to reach her psychically, you may ask her to run a pendulum for you. Call her into your energy before asking your pendulum questions. You will become fascinated by the things she tells you, and the love she radiates will fill your life with blessings and with joy. Always remember that she is you, a greater part of who you are.

In this meditation, which is a short one, you will ask the Lords of Karma to fuse your Energy Selves into one—the one that is called your Light Body. Do the first step as all one process, asking for all the fusions at once rather than one at a time. Simply read the meditation as your request. It is extremely important to do it correctly, and to use the exact given wording. When you receive a "yes," or are not stopped through the first step, go on to the second. Ask the Lords of Karma to take the Energy Self fusions through the Outer Levels (Mind Grid, DNA, Karmic Contract, and Core Soul level and beyond). Ask that the healing be extended from below the center of the Earth to beyond your Moment of Self, and that it be sealed unto the Light and unto protection forever. If you receive a "no" at any point, ask what is needed to release it and do so.

The next request to the Lords of Karma is not to frighten anyone. In the past, it has been assumed that ascension or enlightenment meant leaving the earthplane forever, or in other words, dying. In Buddhist and other legends, enlightenment frequently comes at the moment of death and the person's body disappears—only the hair and fingernails remain. Those who ascend take their bodies with them. Some books on ascension assume this to be the case in our time, as well. My understanding of the process, however, and the personal proof of my own experience, is that this is no longer so.

Discussions with Brede and the Lords of Karma tell a different story. We who enter ascension are the bodhisattvas of our age. We have not achieved enlightenment for the purpose of leaving here, but so that we can help others. Our job is to bring enlightenment/ascension to the planet so that all people and eventually the Earth herself can raise their vibration to the fifth-dimensional level and beyond. We are creating the evolution of all of our energy components including our physical bodies, but are not leaving our bodies permanently until this lifetime is done. Then, as we have completed our reincarnation requirement by healing more than fifty percent of our karma, we shall see what comes after this life.

The request in step three is to make very sure that your Mind Grid belief system does not contain the instructions that ascension means you may leave immediately. Personal reality is created and contained in the Mind Grid, and this is where all the karmic patterns and cultural belief systems are held. When you work with the Lords of Karma, many negative and limiting beliefs and thought forms are healed, changed, and removed from the Mind Grid. Stating clearly before the Lords of Karma that your definition of ascension does not mean that you are ready to die makes it so. The request asks that you complete your lifetime, and even more importantly, your life path for this incarnation. If you are achieving ascension, you are a healer and Lightworker with an Earth mission. You are stating here your acceptance of who you are as a planetary healer, and your mission will now begin if it hasn't already.

As with the other Essential Energy Balancing® processes, do this one in bed the last thing before sleep, lying flat on your back with arms and legs uncrossed. You may wish to do a Process II energy clearing first. As each request is implemented, the energy moves from your head to your feet, and you will feel other psychic activity as well. The sensations are wonderful, with psychic senses much more heightened than usual. You will feel the Energy Selves merging and joining, and see colors and lights. I had auditory and visual impressions of many angels flying, too busy to stop and talk with me. There was an overall feeling of great joy, and my experience with this meditation was intense bliss and great excitement.

Complete the meditation requests, and then, without getting up or moving, go to sleep. You will experience a night to remember, but still feel balanced and able to cope with daily life in the morning. The sense of well-being continues for several days. When doing energy work after this, you need to ask in only your Goddess Self once the fusion is complete.

PROCESS VIII:

The Third Ascension Process

1. Ask the Lords of Karma to *merge* and *fuse* fully, completely, permanently, and forever your:

   Etheric double with physical level

   Astral Twin with Etheric Double

   Higher Self with Astral Twin

   Essence Self with Higher Self

   Goddess Self with Essence Self

   Goddess with all the above (name them)

   Light beyond Goddess with all the above (name them)

2. Ask for this healing through the Outer Levels (Mind Grid, DNA, Karmic Contract, Core Soul level and beyond), and from below the Center of the Earth to beyond your Moment of Self. Ask that the healing be sealed unto the Light and unto protection forever. (All the levels and all the bodies, etc. is not needed.)

3. Ask the Lords of Karma that you not leave this life or the earth-plane until your full lifetime and life path for this incarnation are completed.

4. Rest with the energy for at least two hours; all night is best. This process needs to be done only once if the full fusion completes. Otherwise, repeat it weekly until the fusion occurs.

Energy Balancing Process IX

I have had women walk out of my workshops in this meditation, and frequently hear a gasp of protest when I introduce the subject. The same women, if they stay with me, always change their tune once they've experienced it. Negative interference, call it evil if you will, exists in the world and is real. While few people would disagree with the idea of evil on Earth, even many advanced healers refuse to believe that it exists on other dimensions or in the psychic world. I have experienced it often enough, however, to know that it does. Even if you disbelieve me, I urge you to go through the process, and you must do so if you wish to complete your Light Body activation with Process X.

Denying acceptance of negative interference may be a human defense mechanism. By refusing to acknowledge evil, we are saved from confronting it or being afraid of it. There are definitely things to fear here, but there is no reason to fear the clearing and healing of all negative interference from your energy. Just by the fact of our many incarnations and all of our experiences in them, we have all picked up negativity along the way. If you are a Lightworker on this planet, you have been-energy-attacked in some way, on some level, in some or many of your lifetimes. If you are human, others have tried to manipulate you consciously or unconsciously at some time, and probably it has happened frequently. Whether you are aware of these things having occurred or not (and I have become very aware), they still exist.

Negative interference causes harm. It blocks the self-determining of your life and free will, and obstructs your ability to manifest your life purpose. If you have experienced repeated bad luck or ill health in your life, negative interference from this life or some other can be the cause. What is sometimes jokingly called "bad karma" may in fact be negative interference, too. Constant depression or agitation, negative thinking or destructive thoughts, physical pain, chronic fatigue, dis-ease, emotional disturbance, and certainly a life that is filled with fear, may be from this source. Negative things done to us remain in our energy, as does suffering, until it is removed or healed. This process attempts to remove as many types of negative interference from your energy as possible. You may see some of them leaving, or be shown the situations that go with them.

I have discussed alien implants earlier in this book, and they are only one form of negative interference. Negative entities can attach to your energy in this life and can even be carried over from past incarnations. These are usually people who die but refuse to leave Earth, and they attach to a host to continue having a body here. They may not have been negative people when they were alive, but they are often low-level, and they do not belong in your energy. Sudden personality change often goes with this type of attachment, which is also called possession. This type of entity is rampant and easily picked up in funeral homes, hospitals, and bars, and people who do alcohol or drugs to excess may bring them to you in their energy. They are psychic parasites that can cause great harm. Nonhuman entities that behave similarly are called attachments, and these can include nature elementals. These usually are not evil in themselves, but they are in the wrong place and wreak havoc. The proverbial bull in a china shop is a good analogy.

Karmic pain traps and negative karmic implants are another form of negativity. In a personal experience, it seemed that every time I was close to accomplishing something good in my life, something interfered. I got the chicken pox, or the mentor changed her mind, or I lost the job instead of receiving the promised pay raise. I was very poor at that time and the failures were often desperate. In a healing several years ago, I asked to release these occurrences—which were becoming an obvious pattern—at the Source. This was before I met the Lords of Karma, but the healer I worked with was a good one.

What we were shown looked like a loop or wheel, connected to a man from some forgotten past life. Every time I neared a breakthrough, the wheel flipped me back to where I had started in the situation. I could not go forward, only back. We removed the wheel and sent the man out of my energy, but he only left from the level that we saw. Later, when I discovered that there are many karmic levels, I found the man still operating on other ones. I removed his presence twice more, and thought him gone forever. When I devised Process IX and did it for myself, I found him one more time, hopefully the last. Who knows what karma he may have represented or why he was there to begin with.

Negative manipulation is any act of coercion on any level. Forcing an unwilling person to become your lover by doing spells on him or her is an example. Such spells (and rituals, curses, or negative use of symbols) can exist and remain in your energy unknown to you, from this or other lifetimes. Past-life artifacts are objects that remain in your energy from other incarnations. Some of these can be positive, and most were positive in their own time, but they may not be useful now. I had a ruby necklace in a Russian lifetime that was the symbol of my frustration at being a bored, upper-class woman kept inactive at home. When I asked to release negative artifacts, I discovered it, and removing the necklace also helped to remove some this-life frustration. A woman I did healing with was strangled in a past life, and the strand of barbed wire she was strangled with remained in her energy. Removing it ended her recurrent sore throats and inability to speak out.

Psychic attacks are similar to physical attacks, but happen on other dimensional levels. I did a lecture series in Oregon once and two born again Christian women came to every lecture to harass me. They told me they were praying for my death. I began to experience physical and emotional symptoms from that time that I did not associate with the women. In a healing several years later, however, I found what looked like an arrow with a string connected to it in my solar plexus. When I asked where it came from, I got a clear picture of these women whom I hadn't thought about in years. Removing the arrow made me feel better in many ways thereafter. Energy attacks can be a form of negative alien interference or can come from sources on Earth. They can cause serious Core Soul damage on many levels and can be brought forward from the past and into future lifetimes.

The last example of negative interference is negative mass consciousness energy. We are all products of the belief systems of the planet, as well as the belief systems we have been taught by our cultures and families. If you know that something is wrong there is no need to accept it, but most mass consciousness beliefs are never examined. They are just there, it's just the way it is, and you never think to question it. It is time for many of these cultural beliefs to be looked at and changed, however. War, violence, and racism are examples. By changing such beliefs in your own thinking, you change them in your Mind Grid, thereby changing your karma by changing your mind. In doing this, you also change a piece of the Earth Grid, the planet's mass consciousness. We have a lot of work to do on this one.

In the meditation that follows, you will ask the Lords of Karma to remove this list of negativity and all that is evil from your energy. The Negative Form is my term for the source of all evil, on Earth and many other planets. Take the healing through all the levels. Do the entire list, rather than one item at a time. The levels included in this process are greater than are usually asked for in a Lords of Karma process, in an attempt to clear the interference from every aspect of our Be-ings. Next, you will ask the Lords of Karma to remove all access to your energy of all the forms of negativity. Once this is done through all the levels, the rest of the meditation asks the Lords of Karma for complete protection from further interference.

PROCESS IX:

Core Soul Protection

1. A. Ask the Lords of Karma for complete removal from your energy of all negative interference, including the items on the list below. Ask for them all, all at once.

   negative entities
   negative attachments
   negative elementals
   negative alien influence
   negative alien implants
   negative karmic implants
   negative karmic pain traps
   negative manipulation
   negative rituals, spells, curses, and symbols
   negative past-life artifacts
   all psychic attacks
   all energy attacks
   negative mass consciousness energy
   the Negative Form
   negative energy of all types
   all sources of evil

   B. Ask for the above healing through the list below:

   the Outer Levels (Mind Grid, DNA, Karmic Contract, Core Soul level and beyond)
   from beyond your Moment of Self to below the center of the Earth
   annihilate (the negatives) at your Moment of Self
   past/present/future
   all dimensions and alternate realities
   all the chakras and chakra complexes on all levels
   all the levels and components of your Be-ing
   fully, completely, permanently, and forever
   all the levels and all the bodies, etc.

2. Ask the Lords of Karma for complete removal of all access to your energy by the above negatives. (Do parts A and B.)

3. Ask the Lords of Karma for complete protection of your energy from all the negatives above. Take the healing through the Outer Levels, Moment of Self, past/present/future, all dimensions and alternate realities, all the chakras and chakra complexes, all the levels and components of your Be-ing, fully completely, permanently, and forever. Ask that the healing be sealed unto the Light and unto protection forever. Ask for it through All the levels and all the bodies, etc.

4. Ask the Lords of Karma to assign one or more guardian angels to protect you from energy attacks and evil of all types (no outer levels needed).

>   Ask to meet your angel
>   Ask her name
>   Ask your angel for total protection
>   Talk with your angel for a while

5. Ask the Lords of Karma to fill you with the Radiance of the Light Beyond the Goddess through all the levels and components of your Be-ing. Ask to be filled with so much Light that no evil or negativity may exist, remain, or enter your energy. (No outer levels are needed for this.)

6. Thank the Lords of Karma and your angel. Rest with the energy overnight, or for as long as possible.

Energy Balancing Process X

This is the last process in the Essential Energy Balancing® series and by far the most exciting. The meditation completes the merging and fusion of your Energy Selves, and the full activation of their merging into one as your Light Body. Your Light Body is your full fifth-dimensional Self. After this is completed, many permanent changes occur in your Core Soul energy structures. The process is called ascension and it permanently joins your Goddess Self with your daily life conscious awareness. She will begin to take part in your everyday activities and to influence them, always for the better. She is someone to talk with and to share with, and who will bring more blessings than you can now imagine into your Be-ing.

For a very few women, your Goddess Self will step aside so your Goddess may enter and join with you instead. I am told that this will happen only for one in five hundred women who complete the Energy Balancing process, and it will happen for women only. Occasionally a couple will bring in a Goddess together.

When you bring in a Goddess, you must clear more than seventy-five percent of your Earth karma for your Goddess to be able to enter and remain permanently with you. For those who bring in their Goddess Self, more than fifty percent of karma must be cleared. The additional karmic release makes the ascension process with a Goddess much harder and more difficult. Only those women who are able to accept the severity of the initiation will be chosen to bring in the Goddess energy. The Goddesses are joining with us because it is time to heal the planet, and time for them to walk the Earth again.

About three weeks after completing Process X, you will enter a six-month or longer period of initiation, clearing, and energy repatterning. This is not an easy time, though I have been promised that it will be easier for others than it was for me. I have always been an energy experiment for the Goddess, but the trial and error stage stops here. In this period, all of the karma you have released is removed from your cellular structure. Each energy body is shut down in turn and the complete rewiring and repatterning needed for your energy to contain your Goddess Self or Goddess occurs. You may suffer intermittent periods of deep emotion; this may mean overwhelming pain, fear, anger, or depression, or feelings of abandonment or aloneness. There will be one early period of seven to ten days and nights of this emotional release, and other lesser ones. While the energy bodies are shut down, you will also be out of contact with your guides, Goddess Self, and the Lords of Karma, and so must go through it alone.

The best advice I can offer is to accept it and go through it—the results are very much worth it. These six months are a journey to the Underworld, a testing, and a death and rebirth initiation. Understand what is happening and wait for it to end. Be gentle with yourself while the process is going on. You may wish to be alone more, to sleep more, to eat particular foods (indulge in them unless they are harmful to you). Be sure to drink lots of pure water.

Those around you may not understand what is happening, and even while needing their support you may have to reassure them. You will come through the testing eventually, as a Be-ing of greater Light and far greater joy. A few weeks of difficulty is worth it to heal your karma and join permanently with your Goddess Self or Goddess. If you have been drawn to purchase this book and to go through the meditations, you are probably ready for what will come. You will be protected every step of the way.

This last Energy Balancing process can be done only after you have completed all the preceding meditations. You will not be permitted to do Process X until you are fully ready for the activation, and this is for your own highest good. If the Lords of Karma tell you "no" at any point, stop immediately. This is very important. If this happens, ask the Lords of Karma what is needed for your readiness and follow their instructions. Ask if you may clear the "no" right now, or if you must wait longer to do the activation. If you must wait, continue working with the earlier meditations until you are granted permission for this one. Once you have completed the Light Body Activation, you will usually not need to repeat it, and the changes in your energy will begin immediately.

Do the meditation exactly as given, reading it word for word as you go. It will move very quickly and take only a few minutes to finish. With the final request, for gentle and easy integration, ask that the completion of the healing on all levels happen in the *BEST POSSIBLE NOW*—instead of the usual immediate NOW. This is to slow the process to what is easiest and most comfortable for you.

PROCESS X:

Light Body Activation

Do this final process only after working with the rest of the Energy Balancing exercises (in order) over a period of time. If at any point you are told by the Lords of Karma or your Energy Selves that you are not ready to continue, stop the process. This is extremely important. If you are not ready now, you will be later. Continue working with the earlier exercises until you are granted permission to go on.

The following exercise is the last Energy Balancing Process. You need to do it only once if the process completes the first time.

Do this exercise lying in bed, and go to sleep when finished. Remain lying on your back, arms and legs uncrossed. The process will continue all night and for the nights to come, several weeks in all.

1. Do a complete energy clearing (Process II or V).

2. Ask your Higher Self, Essence Self, and Goddess Self to clear and activate all of your templates and merge and anchor in with you through your Astral Twin, Etheric Double, and Physical levels.

3. Ask your Higher Self, Essence Self, and Goddess Self to clear, heal, and fill your chakras and channels on all levels.

4. Ask your Goddess to merge and anchor in with you through all the levels and components of your Be-ing.

5. Ask your Goddess Self if she is fully fused with your Essence Self. If the answer is "no," ask her to fuse or otherwise follow her instructions. If "yes," go to the next step.

6. Ask your Essence Self if she is fully fused with your Higher Self. If the answer is "no," ask her to fuse or otherwise follow her instructions. If "yes," go to the next step.

7. Ask your Higher Self if she is fully fused with your Astral Twin. If the answer is "no," ask her to fuse or otherwise follow her instructions. If "yes," go to the next step.

8. Ask your Astral Twin if she is fully fused with your Etheric Double. If the answer is "no," ask her to fuse or otherwise follow her instructions. If "yes," go to the next step.

9. Ask your Etheric Double if she is fully fused with your physical levels. If the answer is "no," ask her to fuse or otherwise follow her instructions. If "yes," go to the next step.

   You may need to ask for this over a period of time before all the Energy Selves are fully fused and you get a "yes" to every question. Only when they are, continue the process:

10. Ask the Lords of Karma to anchor in and activate your fused Goddess Self, Essence Self, Higher Self, Astral Twin, Etheric Double, and physical levels as your Light Body. Ask for the healing through the Outer Levels (Mind Grid, DNA, Karmic Contract, Core Soul level and beyond), from below the center of the Earth to beyond your Moment of Self, and ask that the healing be sealed unto the Light and unto protection forever. Ask for it through all the levels and all the bodies, etc.

11. When you feel the energy reach your feet, ask your Light Body her name (it's usually the name of your Goddess Self), and talk with her a while.

12. Ask your activated Light Body to clear, heal, and fill all the levels and components of your Be-ing, fully, completely, permanently, and forever.

13. Ask the Lords of Karma and your Light Body for gentle and easy integration of this healing on all levels and completion in the BEST POSSIBLE NOW.

14. Thank the Lords of Karma and your Light Body. Rest with the energy all night.

15. This is only the beginning…

CORE
SOUL
STRUCTURE

The Physical and Etheric Bodies

I almost hesitate to undertake this section, as our energy systems are so complex and I feel I have so little understanding. Brede, however, has been channeling charts and diagrams through me over the last year and a half, and the material is so fascinating that I need to share it to the best of my ability. The more I learn about soul structure in the development of Essential Energy Balancing®, the more I want to know. We have gone beyond the point where healing through the seven Kundalini chakras is enough. The human (and animal) energy system goes far beyond the Kundalini level and needs healing far beyond it. After hundreds of lifetimes in Earth incarnation, we need healing for our Core Souls.

Most people know about the four bodies, the physical, emotional, mental, and spiritual levels. The first three of these are the closer-to-physical levels. The Core Soul begins beyond the spiritual body. Each of these bodies is a band of energy reaching from our dense physical levels outward. It is hard to describe human energy as up and down or higher and lower, but these are the easiest ways to make the bodies understandable. Our bodies are layers of energy processes. Perhaps deeper is a better explanation than higher, or further from the physical.

Each of the four bodies has a higher octave of energy, a mirror of the lower octave on the next higher vibrational level. Again, higher and lower are not strictly accurate, but are the clearest means of description. These are Core Soul levels. The higher octave of the physical body is the etheric body. The higher octave of the emotional body is the astral level, and the mental body's higher octave is the Mind Grid. The higher octave of the spiri-

DIAGRAM 2

The Templates and Energy Bodies

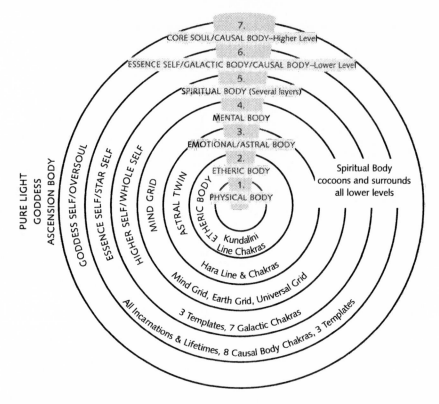

Templates

1. KA		Connects physical body to etheric body, connects Root and Perineum chakras
2. ETHERIC		Connects etheric body to emotional/astral body, connects Heart and Thymus
3. KETHERIC		Connects emotional body to mental body, connects Throat and Causal Body chakras
4. CELESTIAL		Connects mental body to spiritual body, connects Crown and Transpersonal Point chakras
5. I-AM		Connects spiritual body to Higher Self, Essence Self, Goddess Self/Oversoul; Core Soul, connects via the galactic body and chakras (beyond the body entirely)
6. GALACTIC (3)		Brings the Essence Self to Higher Self, connects galactic body to the causal body
7. CAUSAL BODY (3)		Brings the Goddess Self/Oversoul in, connects Goddess Self to Essence Self, connection with Goddess

tual body is the causal body, which is divided into two layers. The lower causal is called the galactic body, while the higher layer is called the causal itself. Anything beyond the spiritual body is mostly uncharted ground until now, and other healers may use different names than the ones in this book. I once asked how many energy bodies we actually have and was told that there are fifty-five primary ones, with more on levels beyond comprehension or reach. These usually are grouped in sets or octaves.

The templates connect the energy bodies, and the Grounding Cord runs through them. The templates are doorways between levels, and when you open and clear them in Essential Energy Balancing® you feel their sensations in the Throat chakra and Crown as they move through the physical and etheric bodies. The five primary templates in order are the Ka, Etheric, Ketheric, Celestial, and I-AM. The Ka Template connects the physical to the etheric body. It anchors into the Kundalini Root chakra and connects that chakra to the Hara Line's Root (the Perineum) on the emotional body. If the Ka Template, or any template, is closed or obstructed, the Energy Selves cannot enter your closer-to-physical energy. The Etheric Template is the doorway from the etheric body to the emotional body. It anchors into the Kundalini Heart chakra through the Hara Line Thymus, and connects the emotional and etheric bodies through these chakras.

The Ketheric Template is the entrance between the emotional body and the mental. It connects the Kundalini Throat chakra to the Hara Line causal body chakra, and to octaves of causal body chakras on other levels. The Celestial Template is the doorway between the mental and spiritual bodies. It connects the Kundalini Crown with the Hara Line Transpersonal Point chakra on the emotional body. The doorway between the spiritual body and the galactic (lower causal) body is the I-AM Template. This is the beginning of the Core Soul levels, and the access point for the Higher Self, Essence Self, and Goddess Self to enter the lower body octaves.

In the lower causal body, there are three Galactic Templates and seven galactic chakras. The Galactic Templates connect the lower and higher causal body levels, and through them the Essence Self connects to the Higher Self. There are three Causal Body Templates and eight chakras on the higher Causal level. These bring in the Goddess Self/Oversoul. This level connects the Goddess Self with the Essence Self below it and the Goddess above it. The I-AM, Galactic, and Causal Body Templates and levels are beyond the closer-to-physical bodies and are door-ways to the Core Soul. When I asked how many templates there really are in human energy, I was told twenty-five to begin with. Again these are in sets and octaves; they connect the bodies.

The Grounding Cord runs through the templates and through physical/etheric energy. The lowest reach of the Grounding Cord is through the Kundalini Line itself, containing the seven chakras most people know, and below them to beyond the center of the Earth. This central channel, where it passes through the Kundalini Line, is known in India as the Sushumna. The furthest outer reach of the Grounding Cord and system is called the Galactic Cord and extends to the Moment of Self, from as far in human energy as can be defined. It runs through all the outer templates, as well. The Grounding system extends through all the levels and all the bodies, and all the chakras and chakra systems on all levels are connected to it.

A set of chakras in the feet, that I have named the Grounding Complex, connects the Grounding Cord to the center of the Earth and beyond on the level of the etheric body. Chakras for each of the closer-to-physical bodies are located in the feet as part of the Grounding Complex and system. On the bottoms of each heel are Grounding Cord connections to the spiritual body, and the tips of the toes are Grounding Cord connections to the mental level. On the sole of each foot is a pair of chakras, one from the emotional body Hara Line (Grounding chakras) and the Earth chakras that are usually considered part of the Hara Line (as the Earth Star below the feet), but are on both the emotional and etheric bodies.

DIAGRAM 3

The Grounding Cord

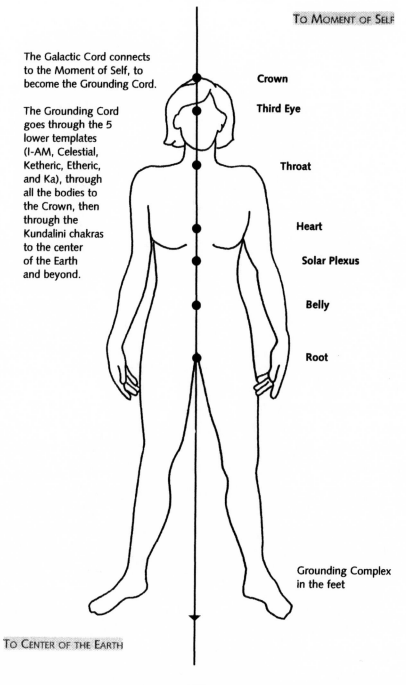

TO MOMENT OF SELF

The Galactic Cord connects to the Moment of Self, to become the Grounding Cord.

The Grounding Cord goes through the 5 lower templates (I-AM, Celestial, Ketheric, Etheric, and Ka), through all the bodies to the Crown, then through the Kundalini chakras to the center of the Earth and beyond.

Crown

Third Eye

Throat

Heart

Solar Plexus

Belly

Root

Grounding Complex in the feet

TO CENTER OF THE EARTH

DIAGRAM 4

The Grounding Complex

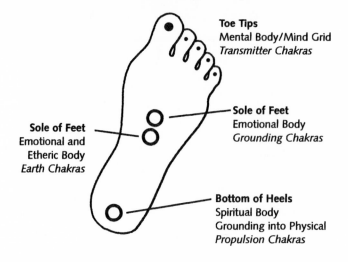

Toe Tips
Mental Body/Mind Grid
Transmitter Chakras

Sole of Feet
Emotional Body
Grounding Chakras

Sole of Feet
Emotional and
Etheric Body
Earth Chakras

Bottom of Heels
Spiritual Body
Grounding into Physical
Propulsion Chakras

All the energy bodies (Physical/Etheric, Emotional, Mental, Mind Grid, and Spiritual) have chakra outlets in the bottoms of the feet.

Each body on each energy level contains a set of chakras. Chakras are energy centers and vortexes; they are transformers that step down higher-octave energy into the level below it. The chakras on the closer-to-physical octave of energy bodies usually mirror those on the outer Core Soul octave, and some of the outer-octave chakras connect into the lower octave of energy. For example, several Mind Grid chakras are also energy connections to the mental body, and some of these have outlets in the Kundalini Line, through the Crown, Third Eye, Solar Plexus, and Root. On the diagrams, it may look like they are the same chakras, but they are on different vibrational levels. This occurs with the physical and etheric levels, emotional and astral levels, mental and Mind Grid chakras, and the spiritual and causal body chakras (two levels).

The physical body contains the dense physical level, what we can see and touch, and a physical aura body. Because the physical aura level is so closely joined with the etheric body, the

DIAGRAM 5

The Human Chakra Systems

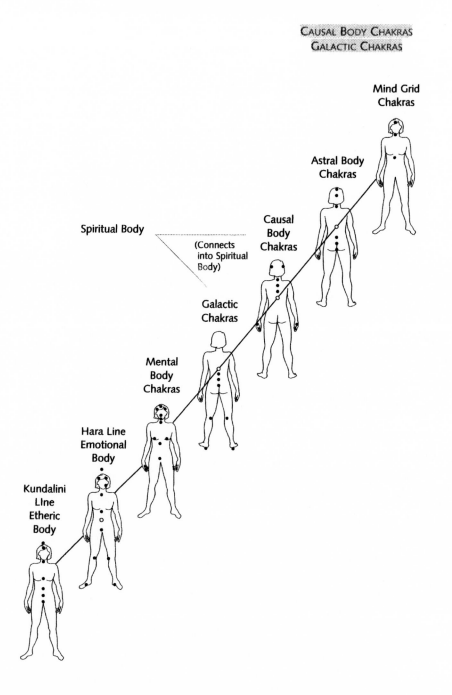

CAUSAL BODY CHAKRAS
GALACTIC CHAKRAS

Mind Grid
Chakras

Astral Body
Chakras

Spiritual Body

Causal
Body
Chakras

(Connects
into Spiritual
Body)

Galactic
Chakras

Mental
Body
Chakras

Hara Line
Emotional
Body

Kundalini
LIne
Etheric
Body

two are often confused. The etheric body, however, is a shadow of the physical body aura, which in turn is a mirror of the dense physical earthplane body. The chakras are so closely joined, since the bodies so closely duplicate, that they are taken as one chakra system. Think of the etheric chakras as also the physical aura body chakras, and both as duplicates or twins of the dense physical earthplane body. The Etheric Twin or Double is located at this level, and is the first of the Energy Selves. Anything that happens in the dense physical body happens first in the physical body aura and the etheric body.

The physical/etheric chakras are the Kundalini Line of seven chakras most people are familiar with. As spirituality and metaphysics are being popularized in the West, most people know something about this chakra series. The Kundalini Line consists of: the Crown chakra (at the top of the head), Third Eye chakra (between and above the physical eyes), Throat chakra (center of the throat), Heart chakra (behind the breast bone), Solar Plexus chakra (at the level of the lower ribs), Belly chakra (at the navel), and Root chakra (pubic bone area, or coccyx at the back). Each chakra has a designated color and sound, and has coordinates to specific areas of physical function.

There are many books and other excellent information on the Kundalini chakras, and as they are readily available, I will discuss these chakras only briefly. The Kundalini Line in humans runs vertically down the front and back of the body along the spinal column. The Kundalini chakras on the back are rarely very open, and they are sealed in the center of the body to prevent their opening from front to back. These seals are released during the ascension process, and the chakras then are opened all the way through the body.

The *Root chakra*, located above the genitals (the tailbone at the back), regulates earthplane life force energy, physical identity, grounding, and survival. Its color is red, and it is the reduced central outlet for the energy octave of the etheric body, which creates the physical aura and dense physical levels.

DIAGRAM 6

The Kundalini Chakras

ETHERIC BODY

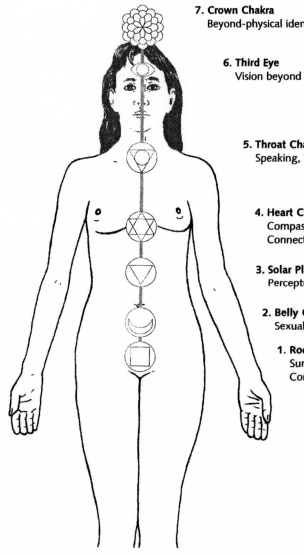

7. Crown Chakra
Beyond-physical identity

6. Third Eye
Vision beyond 3-D

5. Throat Chakra
Speaking, Truth

4. Heart Chakra
Compassion,
Connectedness

3. Solar Plexus Chakra
Perceptual feeling

2. Belly Chakra
Sexuality, Creativity

1. Root Chakra
Survival,
Core identity

Working with the Root always means healing physical earth-plane energy and the Earth incarnation.

The *Belly chakra*, located below the navel, regulates creativity, sexuality, sensuality, and fertility, and is orange in color. It is the reduced physical connection for the energy of the emotional body. Its emotional body mirror, the Hara chakra on the Hara Line, houses one's life purpose for this incarnation.

The third chakra, placed between the lowest ribs, is the *Solar Plexus*. Its color is yellow, and it is the most reduced energy outlet of the mental body, stepped down in turn from the Mind Grid octave above it. This chakra is associated with the conscious mind, rational thought processes, and psychic perception and reception. It is the energy distribution center for the Kundalini system. An individual's earliest psychic perceptions come via the Solar Plexus. As psychic abilities develop, this changes to reception through the Crown and Third Eye, all of which connect to the mental body and Mind Grid.

Next is the *Heart chakra*, found at the center of the breastbone and denoted by the colors of green or pink. The heart chakra brings in the lowest energy octave of the astral body, and connects to the Hara Line (emotional body chakras) through the Hara Line Thymus chakra above it. The Astral Twin is housed at this pair of etheric and emotional body chakras, and the other Energy Selves enter at the back of the heart through the Silver Cord. The Heart and Thymus chakras are a part of the Heart Complex, with chakras connecting to all of the bodies. This is the center for compassion and universal love, and for feeling oneself in union with all others. Most Heart energy is beyond the Kundalini Line, and the Heart chakra is the most reduced outlet (lowest in vibration) for a highly complex energy system. During the completion of the ascension process, the Heart expands to encompass all of the Kundalini chakras.

The light blue *Throat chakra* at the front of the physical throat is the first of three much-lowered energy outlets for the spiritual body. This chakra regulates one's ability to express truth, artistic creation, and to receive psychic speech (empathy). It is the most complex of the chakras because it contains a complete blueprint of the physical, emotional, mental, and spiritual bodies within it, all of which have chakra connections through it. The Throat Complex is perhaps the most intricate of the chakra complexes and the most spectacular to open in the Essential Energy Balancing® process. Energy from the templates is felt in the Throat, though the templates enter the Kundalini Line through the Crown.

The next spiritual body Kundalini chakra is the *Third Eye*, located at the center of the forehead above the physical eyes. This chakra is given the color indigo, or midnight blue. The Third Eye regulates psychic vision, telepathy, and clairvoyance, and is also one of the stepped-down connections of the mental body and Mind Grid chakras in the octaves above it. Our perceptions of what is real are stored in this chakra, and are fed to us from the mental body, Mind Grid, and Earth Grid. These outer octaves of the Third Eye are where our belief systems and mental consciousness originate.

The third spiritual body chakra is located slightly behind the top of the head, and is called the *Crown chakra*. This chakra is usually described as violet in color, and as the seat of beyond-physical consciousness and spirituality. All Core Soul healing work involving Energy Balancing, the templates, DNA reconnection, and ascension reaches the closer-to-physical energy system through this chakra. In the ascension completion process, when the Silver Cord is phased out, astral travel becomes multidimensional teleportation through the Crown.

Each of these chakras is only the physical level outlet for a far more complicated chakra complex. Closest to the physical body, the Kundalini system is also the weakest of the chakra systems, since Core Soul energy must be lowered so drastically to fit into physical energy without damaging it. The chakra complexes each contain connections from all of the energy bodies that we know of, and probably many that we don't. There are at least seventy-two chakras in each chakra complex, a hundred and eight in the Heart Complex, yet most of these have physical connections and dense physical effects.

The chakras on each increasing energy body contain a higher vibration than those on the level below them. Each octave mirrors the one below it but with increased frequency. The physical body chakras and etheric chakras are very close to each other, but this is less true on other levels. The astral body chakras have outlet in the emotional body, but in reduced form; the Mind Grid chakras are reduced in the mental body; and the galactic and causal body chakras are vibrationally higher and stronger than those on the spiritual body level. Each of these bodies' chakras has some outlet on the Kundalini Line, but it is only very limited.

The Energy Self of the etheric body is the Etheric Double. She is a pre-verbal infant, with sensory awareness but little thinking or emotional consciousness. The Etheric Double is a good metaphor for the physical/etheric levels, in that these levels in their two-strand DNA function are so far reduced as to be barely functional. They are all we have had, however, until now.

The Emotional and Astral Bodies

The emotional body is the next level beyond the physical/ etheric, and the astral body is its outer octave. Chakra systems on both of these levels are complex and highly developed, and healers are beginning to understand and work with them. When people think of the emotional body they think of the heart, and the Heart Complex is a series of chakras that bring the energy of all the bodies into the emotional level and connect the bodies to the physical. The hands are an extension of the Heart Complex. The astral body is the higher octave of the emotional body level, and the astral body chakras are anchor points for the Energy Selves. The Astral Twin is the Energy Self for this level. The Etheric Template connects the etheric body to the emotional body, and the Ketheric Template connects the emotional to the mental body.

The emotions are central in karmic healing and in the healing of all Earth karma. Our main reason for incarnating on Earth is to learn to love unconditionally, and most of our karma involves our relationships with the people we love or who love us. These relationships are not only about mates and lovers, but about children and parents, friends, pets, employees and bosses, and also about anyone who has hurt or betrayed our love emotionally or physically. Our love is involved with others' love in every way, and is a testing ground for our ability to give and receive this emotion. Much of the reason for incarnating is to learn what love is and how to do it. The least regarded but probably most important lesson on loving is in learning how to love ourselves.

Most people have damage to their emotional and astral bodies, and this means damage to our ability to love and be loving. We have been hurt again and again through our countless incarnations, and most of the hurts remain unhealed. Emotional damage begins in the etheric Heart chakra. If an emotional hurt is not readily cleared there, it becomes a heart scar, which if not healed moves deeper to affect the emotional body level. If the damage is severe, it moves into the astral body (outer octave of the emotional body), where it is stored and becomes even harder to release. If unhealed in the lifetime where the damage originated, the hurt becomes part of the astral makeup of the next incarnation. From this point it can be transmitted into further lifetimes and becomes karmic damage, and will recur until it is released. This may mean experiencing a same or similar situation or person in another lifetime for the opportunity to return to the situation and resolve it. Emotional hurt that remains uncleared over more than one lifetime becomes a karmic pattern whose healing is increasingly difficult.

The other focus of the emotional body is that of life purpose. We enter each incarnation with a specific set of goals that become our life's work and life path. Often these goals involve service to others or the planet, and they are the highest expression of who we are and of our positive karma. Karma is so often considered negative, but it is important to remember that benefits reincarnate as well as difficulties, and we never lose the evolution we have gained. Our life purpose and life path are part of our pre-incarnation agreements with the Lords of Karma. The drive to complete these goals and agreements is programmed into the emotional body. Unless we have a desire to accomplish something, we will have no reason or impetus to do it. Strong connections to the planet are also located at the emotional body level, and we are anchored to the center of the Earth through the emotional and etheric bodies.

The emotional body has a highly developed set of chakras, on a higher energy vibration than those of the etheric Kundalini Line. These are called the Hara Line, and they contain thirteen chakras along the vertical center of the body, with their energy moving down the front and up the back. Though on a different energy level, the Hara chakras are located on the body between the Kundalini chakras. Their two energy channels, when connected in Ch'i Kung or Yoga practice, move in a circle through the body called the Great Cosmic Orbit. In India these channels are erroneously ascribed to the Kundalini Line, and they are called the Ida and Pingala there.

The Grounding Cord runs in a direct line through the three key Hara Line chakras—the Transpersonal Point, Hara chakra, and Earth Star. These become our stabilization anchors into planet Earth. (Though the Grounding Cord runs through all the Hara Line chakras, these are the major anchors.) Several chakras that have the purpose of grounding us into the incarnation, the Earth, and our life paths are contained on the Hara Line and run through and below it. These include the Perineum chakra, which is the emotional body equivalent to the root; a pair of Movement chakras behind the knees; a pair of Grounding chakras in the soles of the feet; and the Earth chakra or Earth Star below the body.

The Hara Line chakras are as follows, moving from head to feet. First is the *Transpersonal Point* or Soul Star, the emotional body equivalent of the etheric Crown. Its color is clear. Located above the Crown and beyond the body, this center is a connection with the Core Soul and with all of our energy components beyond the physical/etheric levels. Though its energy is still reduced, it is higher than that of the Crown, but lower than the many energy systems beyond it. It increases our outreach to the universe and expands who we are, to our Core Soul levels, and to spirituality further than the Crown can take us. Some healers attribute this chakra to the etheric body as an extension of the Kundalini Line, but it is on another level entirely.

Next are the *Vision chakras*, a pair of small chakras behind the eyes, that are silver or gray in color. These are part of the psychic vision system, with the etheric Third Eye and the mental body Light chakras at the temples. These chakras also make

DIAGRAM 7

The Hara Line Chakras

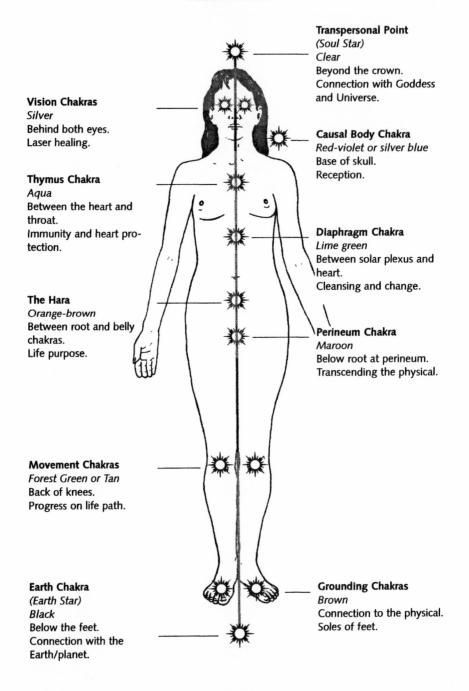

Transpersonal Point
(Soul Star)
Clear
Beyond the crown.
Connection with Goddess
and Universe.

Vision Chakras
Silver
Behind both eyes.
Laser healing.

Causal Body Chakra
Red-violet or silver blue
Base of skull.
Reception.

Thymus Chakra
Aqua
Between the heart and
throat.
Immunity and heart pro-
tection.

Diaphragm Chakra
Lime green
Between solar plexus and
heart.
Cleansing and change.

The Hara
Orange-brown
Between root and belly
chakras.
Life purpose.

Perineum Chakra
Maroon
Below root at perineum.
Transcending the physical.

Movement Chakras
Forest Green or Tan
Back of knees.
Progress on life path.

Earth Chakra
(Earth Star)
Black
Below the feet.
Connection with the
Earth/planet.

Grounding Chakras
Brown
Connection to the physical.
Soles of feet.

it possible for some people to use their eyes as lasers in psychic healing. Even if the Third Eye is open, psychic vision requires these chakras to be open and unobstructed for images to be received.

The *Causal Body chakra* is a sound reception chakra located at the back of the head where the skull meets the neck. It may be silver blue or red-violet in color, and it is part of the Throat Complex. Its purpose is receiving other-than-physical communication and manifesting or translating it into information useful on Earth. It is important in channeling. Other reception and communication chakras on other levels feed into these chakras, although always at reduced energy rates.

The emotional body equivalent of the Heart chakra is the Thymus, sometimes called the High Heart, located above the Kundalini Heart chakra. Its color is aqua or turquoise, and it is the anchor point for the Astral Twin. This center is a protector of the heart and immune system, as immunity and the physical thymus gland are both emotionally directed. Grief and compassion are key emotions for this chakra. On higher levels, the Thymus brings energy from the Silver Cord on the back of the Heart Complex into the emotional system. If the Hara Chakra (below) is the focus wheel for Earth incarnation, the Thymus is the focus of connecting with who we are beyond Earth. The Energy Selves, which enter through the Silver Cord, merge into the emotional body through this chakra.

At the middle of the body, between the etheric Solar Plexus and Heart chakras, is the lime green *Diaphragm chakra*. This is the center that regulates emotional cleansing and the life changes that often follow it. I have heard it called the "garbage chakra" and "vomit chakra," for its function of emotional purging. This detoxification and energy clearing is a way of healing damage and preventing it from deepening or being carried into other lifetimes. Even if the clearing is sometimes uncomfortable, it is still positive and necessary.

The *Hara chakra* is located about two inches below the navel, and it houses one's life purpose and the desire to achieve it. For this reason, it is an extremely important center. It is a frequent site for negative hooks, which are karmic attachments to people who are obstructing your life path. Practitioners of Ch'i Kung call this center the Tan Tien, or the place of Original Ch'i—the store of incarnational life force energy you were born with. Any disruption of this energy has negative consequences in your life. The Hara is the central axis or balance point of the body, and its color is orange-brown, shading to gold brown or almost to red.

The following Hara Line chakras contain the focus of grounding your incarnation into the earthplane, and into the center of the Earth. They also are focused on manifesting your life purpose on the physical plane. If the Hara contains the desire to fulfill your life's work, these chakras bring the desire into manifestation. The first of them is the *Perineum chakra*, the emotional equivalent of the Root. It is located lower on the body than the Kundalini Root chakra, between the vagina and the anus, where episiotomies are done during childbirth. This is the chakra for both transcending the physical and manifesting it, for bringing one's spiritual life purpose into earthplane physicality. In the East, the Perineum chakra is called the gateway of life and death.

A pair of chakras at the back of the knees, the tan or forest green *Movement chakras*, are also part of the grounding system on the emotional body level. These are important for stability and for progress on one's life path. When open and functioning properly, they aid in moving forward for the accomplishment of one's karmic agreements. The brown *Grounding chakras*, on the soles of the feet, are connections to the physical and the earthplane. In conjunction with the Movement chakras, they work to "keep one's feet on the ground" and connected to the planet. The black *Earth chakra* or Earth Star below the feet, which in the first Essential Energy Balancing® process is reconnected to the center of the Earth, is the grounding anchor for your life path. It is intrinsic in manifesting your spiritual purpose for this lifetime, and for every Earth incarnation—past, present, and future.

The Heart Complex is a set of chakras from all levels that come together in the Thymus, the emotional body heart, and radiate through all the closer-to-physical levels. These chakras consist of the etheric Heart, emotional body Thymus, a pair of chakras in the breasts from the mental body, and the Silver Cord on the back of the Heart/Thymus from the spiritual body level. The Heart Complex also includes chakras in the hands: a pair that is connected to the Thymus/emotional body, and a pair that is connected to the physical/etheric Heart. Additional chakras in the hands that are part of this complex are small mental body chakras at the tips of each finger, and a spiritual body chakra on each wrist.

These chakras radiate love to and from all levels of the human energy system. The etheric Heart chakra is uncondi-tional love, and the Thymus is compassionate love. The Silver Cord on the spiritual body transmits universal love, and is the access point where the Energy Selves enter. It brings love from higher dimensions and Goddess. The breasts are sexual and nurturing love, while the chakras in the centers of the palms are for giving love (emotional body) and receiving or accepting love (etheric). The mental body finger tip chakras are transmitters and receivers of sensory perception. Those on the wrists create a back to front energy flow to the hands, and are chakras for work or other implementations of spirit. They are extremely important if you are a hands-on or Reiki healer.

Energy flows from the outer octaves into and through the Heart Complex, and though reduced in vibration, it flows in a specific way. It enters through the Crown and Silver Cord on the back, and the Silver Cord then fills first the Thymus chakra and next the Heart, moving through the thickness of the body. From here the energy moves through the breast chakras in front, and down the arms to the hands. The flow of energy through the Heart Complex is downward only, with the excess

DIAGRAM 8

The Heart Complex

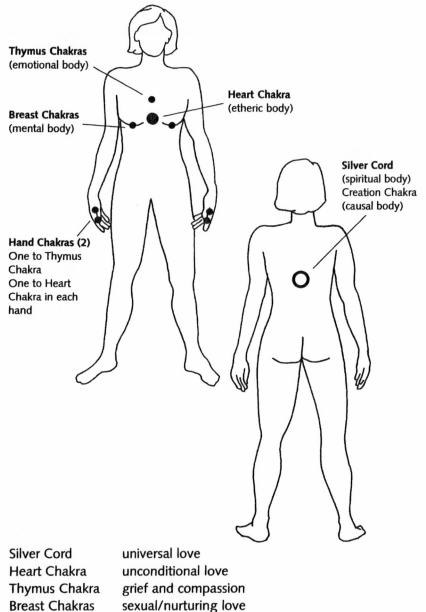

Thymus Chakras
(emotional body)

Heart Chakra
(etheric body)

Breast Chakras
(mental body)

Silver Cord
(spiritual body)
Creation Chakra
(causal body)

Hand Chakras (2)
One to Thymus
Chakra
One to Heart
Chakra in each
hand

Silver Cord	universal love
Heart Chakra	unconditional love
Thymus Chakra	grief and compassion
Breast Chakras	sexual/nurturing love
Hand Chakras	giving and receiving love
(2 each palm)	

The Creation Chakra (causal body) is the opening to the Silver Cord and
Moment of Self.

DIAGRAM 9

Heart Complex Energy Flows

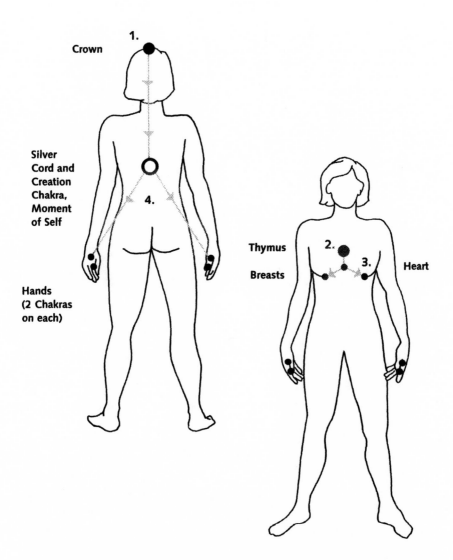

1. Crown to Silver Cord (on back) ➤ 2. Silver Cord fills Thymus Chakra then Heart Chakra (on front) by energy moving through the thickness of the body ➤ 3. Silver Cord fills the breast chakras (in front) ➤ 4. Energy from the Silver Cord moves down back of arms to hands. Flows are downward only. Hand chakras are on the palms (front) of hands.

DIAGRAM 10

The Chakras in the Hands

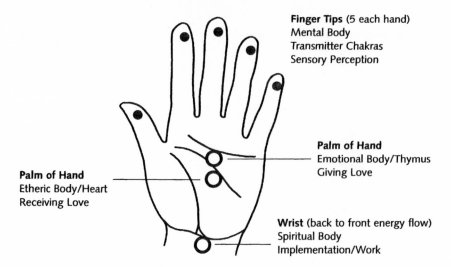

Finger Tips (5 each hand)
Mental Body
Transmitter Chakras
Sensory Perception

Palm of Hand
Emotional Body/Thymus
Giving Love

Palm of Hand
Etheric Body/Heart
Receiving Love

Wrist (back to front energy flow)
Spiritual Body
Implementation/Work

All the energy bodies (Physical/Etheric, Emotional/Astral, Mental, Mind Grid, and Spiritual) have chakra outlets in the palms of the hands.

leaving the body through the feet. We give what we have received through the Thymus, Heart, and hands.

The astral body contains the lowest energy level of the Silver Cord, as well as a series of chakras down the back of the body. These mirror the etheric chakras of the Kundalini Line. At this outer octave level, however, they are access points for the Energy Selves. While all of the Energy Selves enter the closer-to-physical levels through the Silver Cord, each anchors at a different chakra level that is an outlet for the bodies. All of these outlets are on the astral body, the outer octave of the emotional level.

The Infant Self/Etheric Double is anchored at the Astral Root, access point to the etheric level. The Inner Child/Astral Twin anchors into the Astral Belly chakra and emotional body access: it is said that the wounded Inner Child lives in the Belly, while the healed one moves into the Heart. There is no astral equivalent of the Solar Plexus and no Energy Self for it; this is the mental body and Mind Grid, entrance to the Void of all karma and creation, and it bypasses the emotional levels completely. The Maiden/Higher Self is anchored at the Astral Heart chakra, and all the Energy Selves enter here, through the Silver Cord. At the Astral Throat and lower causal body (Galactic body) is the Mother, the Essence Self; at the Astral Third Eye and higher causal body is the Crone/Goddess Self, and the Astral Crown anchors the Three-in-One Goddess from beyond the causal body level.

To summarize, the Energy Selves enter the astral body through the Silver Cord. Each operates in stepped-down form through a chakra on the back of the body. These chakra connections feed the Energy Selves' vibration into the etheric body and through the physical/etheric level. Their energy must be decreased and reduced through each body level to prevent their damaging the closer-to-physical levels and the physical body. Once the DNA is reconnected and reactivated to twelve strands, more of this energy and more contact with the Energy Selves will be possible. Energy enters the Silver Cord, then moves through the Heart Complex, downward to the heels of the feet. It may also move upward from Silver Cord to Crown and beyond, though the Energy Selves do not use this route.

The Astral Twin resides on the astral body level. She is known to many as the Inner Child. In appearance she is usually from six to ten years old, and the healed Astral Twin has wings. She loves to do wheelies in the air or to appear in a different wing style each time she comes. She may also appear as yourself at an earlier age, particularly at an age when there was trauma in your life. When emotional wounding occurs, the Astral Twin receives the pain, and it is this part of your Be-ing that is the most damaged by it.

This emotional Energy Self is fragile and easily fragmented. In response to a shock, a part of her may break off. These parts look like the whole Be-ing, but will remain the age appearance of when the splitting occurred. There can be many of these astral parts or soul fragments, and a particularly severe shattering

DIAGRAM 11

The Astral Body Chakras

THE SILVER CORD AND CHAKRAS DOWN THE BACK

Connections to Energy Selves at Astral Body Level

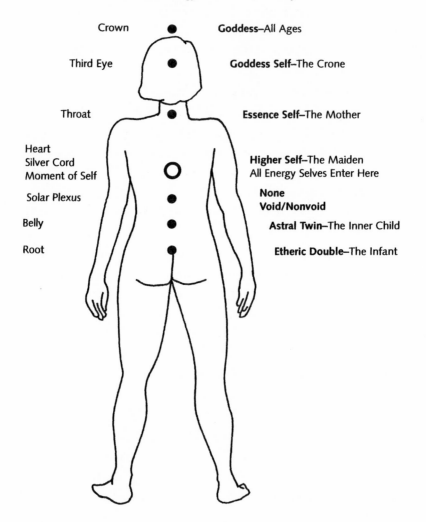

Crown — **Goddess–All Ages**

Third Eye — **Goddess Self–The Crone**

Throat — **Essence Self–The Mother**

Heart
Silver Cord
Moment of Self — **Higher Self–The Maiden**
All Energy Selves Enter Here

Solar Plexus — **None**
Void/Nonvoid

Belly — **Astral Twin–The Inner Child**

Root — **Etheric Double–The Infant**

The Energy Selves enter the Astral Body via the Silver Cord. Each operates in stepped-down form through a primary chakra down the back of the body. These chakra connections feed the Energy Selves' influence into the Etheric Body and then to effect the Physical. Their energy is reduced/stepped down through each body level to prevent their damaging the near-to-physical levels and physical body.

DIAGRAM 12

Astral Body Energy Flows

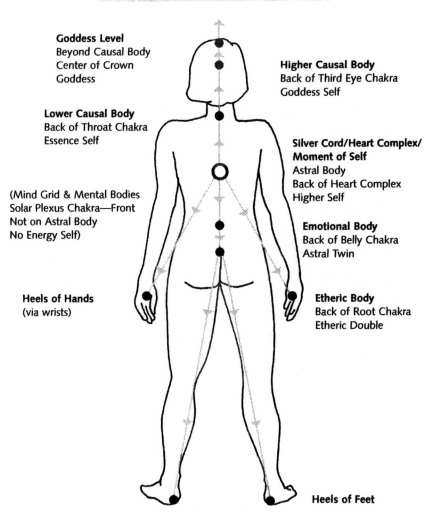

Goddess Level
Beyond Causal Body
Center of Crown
Goddess

Higher Causal Body
Back of Third Eye Chakra
Goddess Self

Lower Causal Body
Back of Throat Chakra
Essence Self

Silver Cord/Heart Complex/
Moment of Self
Astral Body
Back of Heart Complex
Higher Self

(Mind Grid & Mental Bodies
Solar Plexus Chakra—Front
Not on Astral Body
No Energy Self)

Emotional Body
Back of Belly Chakra
Astral Twin

Heels of Hands
(via wrists)

Etheric Body
Back of Root Chakra
Etheric Double

Heels of Feet

Energy from all the bodies passes in stepped-down form through the Astral Body level to anchor into the Etheric Body at the backs of the Kundalini (Etheric Body) chakras. The Mental Body and Mind Grid, however, bypasses the Astral and Emotional Levels completely. Energy from each body and Energy Self enters the Astral Body via the Silver Cord/Back of Heart and moves upward and downward through the chakras. See charts for each body, chakra series, and the Heart Complex.

can result in these fragments becoming multiple personalities. Each split leaves the emotional body a little more damaged and a little more vulnerable to further damage. There may be dozens of soul fragments from many lifetimes. A request to the Lords of Karma in Essential Energy Balancing® is to heal, bring in, and fully integrate all of these fragments. They must be healed before being returned to your energy so as not to regenerate the pain that caused them to leave. They must be integrated fully into your emotional/astral body energy so they do not split off again.

The healed Inner Child/Astral Twin lives in the Heart Complex. She is the innocence, joy, and beauty we were meant to experience as children, and also meant to retain as adults. The wounded Inner Child in the Belly chakra reacts to pain and damage; she receives and expects to receive, repeated emotional hurts. In the heart when she is healed, she gives and receives love instead. These are the attributes of the healed emotional body and its astral higher octave. Healing these levels is a giant step in soul evolution.

The Mental Body and the Mind Grid

What we think is what we are. All reality is in the mind and what we believe comes into physical existence by our thinking it into Be-ing. This is no accident, as the mental body and its outer octave, the Mind Grid, are the computers into which we program what we wish to create and be. The problem is that these computers accept all programming without discrimination. If we think it, it becomes so. If we think something that we don't really want or mean, it still gets programmed in. What we think consciously is programmed, and what we think without awareness or understanding is also programmed in. From this hash we must select a reality we can live with, and make the best of all the confusion that results. It's a wonder we can function at all.

Add to this the programming of our cultures, what we are taught by our families (right or wrong), what we learn in school, from the media, and the tangled web of karma we came into Be-ing with. All of these are found in the programming of our computers—again, without always making sense. There is a "sort" function to this computer, but not a highly developed one, and it only works on the lowest levels and the highest ones—we live somewhere in-between. The computer is our mental bodies, its lower levels are the closer-to-physical chakras the mental body accesses, and its higher levels are the Mind Grid, Earth Grid, and beyond.

Our minds are influenced by the consensus of the planet—that there is time, that there is only one right and wrong (ours), that we are the only sentient Be-ings, that right equals might, that survival comes only to the fittest, that a just war is possible. We are part of the mass consciousness of the Earth, and immersed in its misconceptions and negativity. We believe that life is dangerous, that it results only in suffering, that we are all alone, that we are our physical bodies, and that death is the end of who we are. We believe what we have learned as children, which is what others learned from group consensus, whether or not the concepts are correct or healthy for us as adults.

Our minds store anything we learn from any level. They put no emotional weight or emphasis on one idea over another because the mental levels have no emotion or emotional access. They only have ideas and an obsessive need to program them into the whole. They want to keep everything, just in case we might need it later, and if they keep everything maybe something will make sense or be of use. Often it is, but more often the sheer glut of conflicting ideas results in a reality that is unlivable. We are as frenzied as rats on an exercise wheel. Perhaps it's time to stop thinking and start feeling, to trust instead of to analyze and compute. Perhaps our mental bodies and Mind Grids, and our connection to the mass consciousness of the Earth Grid, need an overhaul, or an attitude adjustment. That would be a great relief.

The way to heal the mental body is to weed out all that is no longer useful. Working with the Lords of Karma is a good way to do that. Another way is to more frequently access our higher emotions instead of our minds. Look inside and notice what feels joyful. Look inside at your fears and notice which are actually real, and where they came from to begin with. Notice your thoughts and do the same. Which are negative without reason? Can you find a negative thought that is truthful and real in the larger picture? If you notice and fill each negative idea with love, you will watch it disappear. Still a further way to sort out the tangle is simply to trust. The Goddess (or whatever you choose to call Source energy) is there and She is real. You are not alone and have never been abandoned. Earth is beautiful, and a place of miracles, after all.

The mental body is the third closer-to-physical level of human and animal energy in Earth incarnation. It follows the physical/etheric and the emotional body levels, and is followed by the spiritual, galactic, and causal bodies. Its outer octave is the Mind Grid, which has several layers and levels of its own, reaching out to beyond our known universe. Mental body chakras connect to the Mind Grid above and the Kundalini Line below them. The Ketheric Template connects the emotional to the mental body, and the Celestial Template connects the mental level to the spiritual. There is no Energy Self at these levels, and as has been described previously, the mental body and Mind Grid are very different from other energy.

There is a chakra system on the mental body, and the chakras on it are mostly involved with sensory perception, seeing, speaking, and recording. Their major question is "what is truth?" There is no emotion on this level, and no emotional body chakra connections. Knowledge is paramount, and the goal is to create a reality that makes sense. This reality must be cobbled together from facts, not emotions, and is more drawn to equations and formulas than to feelings. The mental body works through every level except the emotional and astral.

Among the sensory perceptions on the mental body level is that of psychic perception. The mental body Crown, Third Eye, Light chakras, and Solar Plexus are involved in gathering psychic information and psychic vision. Psychic knowing is accepted on this level, but not psychic feeling (emotional body). Clairaudience (psychic hearing) comes from the spiritual level that is next. Mental body chakras are also involved with the distribution of energy, including electrical and psychic energy through the mental/Mind Grid systems.

I have given the chakras that follow Kundalini names, but it is important to realize that though they have outlet on the Kundalini level, they are not Kundalini etheric chakras. They operate on a much higher vibrational level, and are more accurately parts of Chakra Complexes than etheric chakras. To my knowledge, there are no names for these mental body chakras, and I have used familiar names in an attempt at clarity. Earth has been so cut off from knowing who we are, that these energy systems have become unknown to us. While learning about this energy level, I asked repeatedly for Brede or the Lords of Karma to "show me that again," and they would move the mental body energy through me so I could feel its pathways. Brede once showed me a body outline with little lights, like Christmas tree lights, to mark the chakras so I could understand their positions. I could not determine colors for these chakras.

The mental body chakras begin at the Crown Complex with connection to the spiritual body and Mind Grid. Connection through the Third Eye Complex is next and accesses mental knowing, followed by a pair of chakras at the temples I have named Light chakras that are Mind Grid connections. The Light chakras are a part of the psychic vision system, carrying information from outer levels to bring visual images to the etheric body. Other chakras of the vision system are the emotional body Vision chakras and the etheric Third Eye. Three chakras in the Throat Complex are mental body chakras. These are located at the lips, top of the throat, and lower throat. I have defined them as speaking one's mind (lips), speaking personal truth (top of the throat), and expressing spiritual truth—the connection of body, mind, and spirit—at the lower throat.

Two chakras on the breasts for sexual/nurturing love are mental body components of the Heart Complex and are next. A chakra in the Solar Plexus Complex follows, which connects the mental body to the etheric level. A mental body chakra with access through the Root Complex, like the Solar Plexus chakra, connects the mental body to the etheric level. There are also small chakras on each finger and toe tip (20 in all) that are transmitters of sensory perception. With the fingers and toes, there are thirty-one chakras in all on the mental body.

Two energy flows move simultaneously through this level,

DIAGRAM 13

The Mental Body Chakras

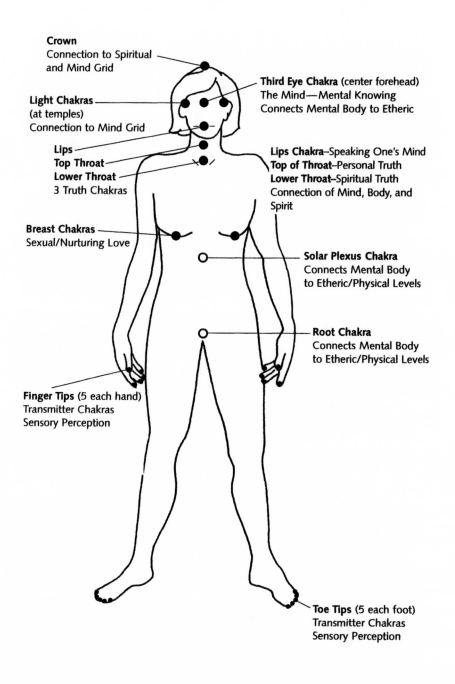

Crown
Connection to Spiritual
and Mind Grid

Third Eye Chakra (center forehead)
The Mind—Mental Knowing
Connects Mental Body to Etheric

Light Chakras
(at temples)
Connection to Mind Grid

Lips
Top Throat
Lower Throat
3 Truth Chakras

Lips Chakra–Speaking One's Mind
Top of Throat–Personal Truth
Lower Throat–Spiritual Truth
Connection of Mind, Body, and
Spirit

Breast Chakras
Sexual/Nurturing Love

Solar Plexus Chakra
Connects Mental Body
to Etheric/Physical Levels

Root Chakra
Connects Mental Body
to Etheric/Physical Levels

Finger Tips (5 each hand)
Transmitter Chakras
Sensory Perception

Toe Tips (5 each foot)
Transmitter Chakras
Sensory Perception

DIAGRAM 14

Mental Body Energy Flows

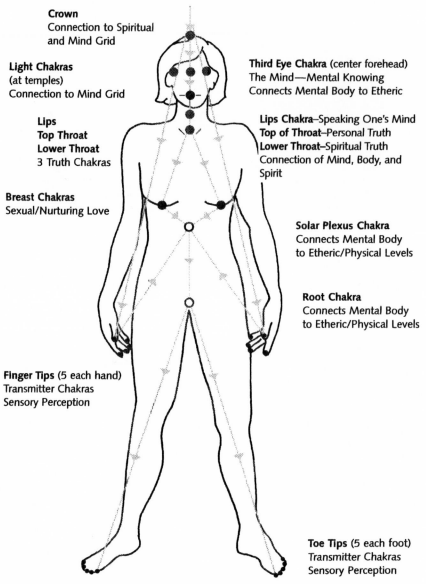

Crown
Connection to Spiritual
and Mind Grid

Light Chakras
(at temples)
Connection to Mind Grid

Lips
Top Throat
Lower Throat
3 Truth Chakras

Breast Chakras
Sexual/Nurturing Love

Finger Tips (5 each hand)
Transmitter Chakras
Sensory Perception

Third Eye Chakra (center forehead)
The Mind—Mental Knowing
Connects Mental Body to Etheric

Lips Chakra–Speaking One's Mind
Top of Throat–Personal Truth
Lower Throat–Spiritual Truth
Connection of Mind, Body, and
Spirit

Solar Plexus Chakra
Connects Mental Body
to Etheric/Physical Levels

Root Chakra
Connects Mental Body
to Etheric/Physical Levels

Toe Tips (5 each foot)
Transmitter Chakras
Sensory Perception

Mental Body—Two energy flows
1) Crown ➤ Third Eye ➤ 3 Throat Chakras ➤ Breast Chakras ➤
Solar Plexus ➤ Root Chakra ➤ Toes
2) Crown ➤ Temples ➤ front of arms ➤ Finger tips ➤ up to
Solar Plexus (joins with flow #1) ➤ Root Chakra ➤ down legs and
toes. Flows move simultaneously down front of body.

DIAGRAM 15

Mental Body Energy Flow I

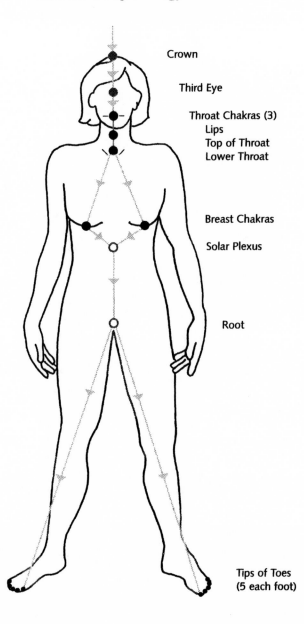

Crown

Third Eye

Throat Chakras (3)
Lips
Top of Throat
Lower Throat

Breast Chakras

Solar Plexus

Root

Tips of Toes
(5 each foot)

Mental Body Energy Flow 1
Crown ➤ Third Eye ➤ 3 Throat Chakras ➤ Breast Chakras ➤
Solar Plexus ➤ Root Chakra ➤ Toes. Energy moves simultaneously
with Energy Flow #2 down front of body.

DIAGRAM 16

Mental Body Energy Flow II

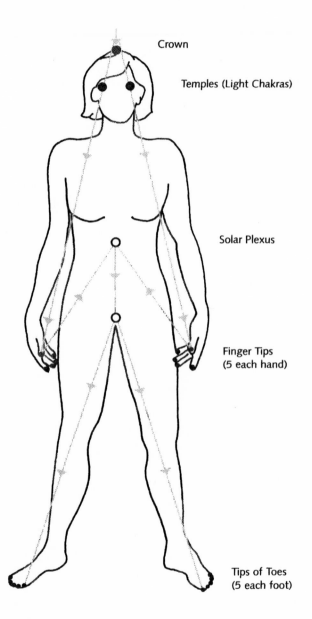

Crown

Temples (Light Chakras)

Solar Plexus

Finger Tips
(5 each hand)

Tips of Toes
(5 each foot)

Mental Body Energy Flow 2
Crown ➤ Temples ➤ down front of arms ➤ finger tips ➤ up to Solar Plexus (joins with Flow #1) ➤ Root Chakra ➤ down legs to toes. Flows move simultaneously down front of body.

both beginning at the Crown. From the Crown, energy moves in the first flow pattern to the Third Eye, the three mental body Throat chakras, the Breasts, Solar Plexus, mental body Root chakra, and finally out through the toe tips. In the second energy pattern, the flow moves from the Crown to the Light chakras at the temples, down the front of the arms to the finger tips, and then to the Solar Plexus where it joins with Flow I. The energy then moves through the Root chakra, and down the legs to exit through the tips of the toes. These energy flows move down the front of the body. They serve to connect the Mind Grid with the spiritual, mental, and etheric bodies, while bypassing the emotional body completely.

The mental body's outer octave is the Mind Grid, one of the most interesting components of Core Soul structure. The Mind Grid seen psychically looks like a screen or mesh of gold wire, shaped like a dome that surrounds the bodies. This is the computer hard drive, where all of thought, belief, and karma are arranged and stored. The Mind Grid has in turn several higher octaves that it plugs into. The first is the Earth Grid, the planet's collective mass consciousness. Next is the Galactic Grid, which is the cooperative consciousness of the galaxy and of all other inhabited planets in it. The last and highest level is the Universal Grid, reflecting the universal consciousness of oneness.

The Mind Grid is called the Void in Buddhist terminology. It is the place of darkness and positive chaos from which all reality is created. Karma is programmed into the Mind Grid and stored there, and its release is a reprogramming. All reality is drawn from the Mind Grid, from the Void. As Nada, who is Keeper of the Earth's Karma—and therefore of our personal Mind Grids—states, "All that is born passes through me." The Mind Grid is the place of all the possibilities and realities that we (literally) can think of. But possibility must also be made manifest.

This happens in the Nonvoid (Buddhist term), which is our mental bodies. Here is where the "sort" function exists, to choose among the countless possibilities and create reality from them. Our limits are created in our minds, in what we think.

The Mind Grid is limitless and the limits we have created can be changed. This is how karma exists and is healed, by changing the Mind Grid through our mental bodies, and through our minds' conscious and unconscious choice to do so.

On a descending level, the personal Mind Grid has chakra connections with its lower octave mental body. The mental body, in turn, with its etheric level chakra input, influences the individual mind (etheric body) and physical brain. Karma works through these levels, in both directions. It becomes programmed into the Mind Grid when a situation moves from physical/etheric levels through the emotional/astral, and into and through the mental body. Once a situation is programmed, it remains part of the Mind Grid through as many incarnations as necessary until the situation is completed or released. When the Lords of Karma grant a release, it happens in the Mind Grid and then filters down through the levels, in reverse order, until it reaches the etheric body. From there the changes may affect the dense physical body as well.

Every piece of personal karma that is cleared also clears a part of the Earth Grid. This grid is collective of what everyone on Earth thinks and believes. Each change in human belief changes the planetary programming. By clearing our karma and raising our vibrational levels while doing so, we also clear and raise the Earth Grid and the planet. Every piece of individual karmic healing is a planetary healing. For every situation there is a critical mass. Beyond that point of clearing and release, something is moved completely out of the Earth Grid and out of human mass consciousness on Earth. Great change can be effected, and it does not take an impossible number of people to do it.

Chakras on the Mind Grid level are stepped down through the mental body, and are then reduced in vibration and energy to enter the etheric level. The energy pathway moves through the Crown Complex (on all spiritual level octaves) to the Creation chakra on the causal body level of the Silver Cord, located at the back of the Heart. From there it flows down the arms and legs, into the mental body finger and toe tips. A

DIAGRAM 17

The Mind Grid Levels

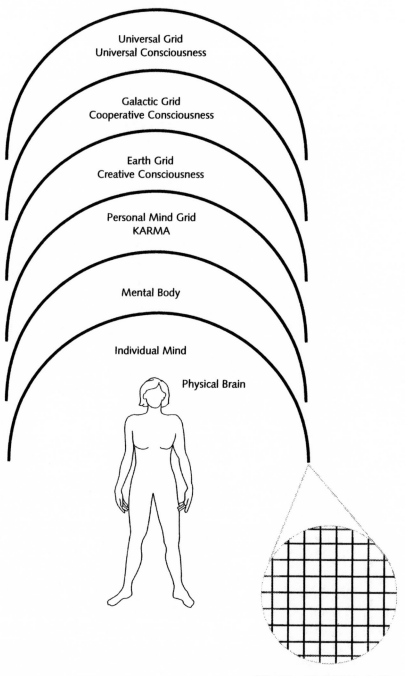

Universal Grid
Universal Consciousness

Galactic Grid
Cooperative Consciousness

Earth Grid
Creative Consciousness

Personal Mind Grid
KARMA

Mental Body

Individual Mind

Physical Brain

What the Mind Grid looks like

DIAGRAM 18

Mind Grid Chakra Energy Flows

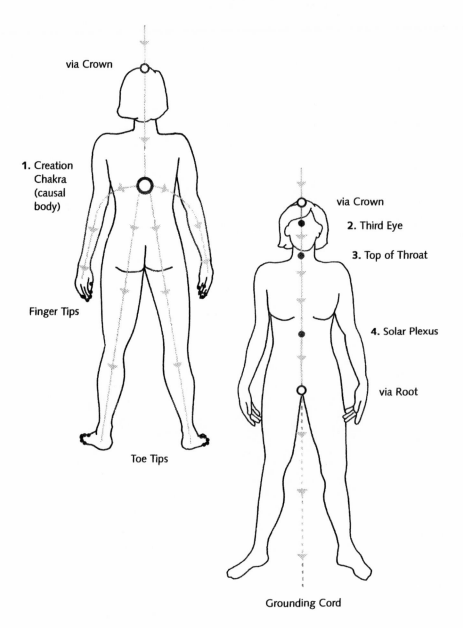

via Crown

1. Creation Chakra (causal body)

Finger Tips

Toe Tips

via Crown

2. Third Eye

3. Top of Throat

4. Solar Plexus

via Root

Grounding Cord

Simultaneous energy flows front and back, moving from head to feet.

second pathway, also entering via the Crown, passes down the front of the body through the etheric Third Eye Complex, the top of Throat chakra, the etheric Solar Plexus, and leaves the body through the Root Complex at the etheric level. These etheric connections are through several levels of the chakra complexes on the front, and from the spiritual, galactic, and causal levels to the mental levels on the back. The energy passes through at least the first five templates, the Galactic Cord, and the Grounding Cord. It moves down front and back of the body simultaneously.

This complicated description is the closest approximation I can channel, and the truth is probably even more complex. We are entering uncharted levels of human energy, at the end of our furthest reach, and I apologize for any errors or lack of fuller understanding. The information above, however, gives a beginning explanation of how energy, as Light and information, reaches our consciousness from the outer components of who we are. To give a point of reference, remember that the Higher Self, Essence Self, Goddess Self, and Goddess are all beyond the Mind Grid. In the Essential Energy Balancing® process, however, they are brought in and anchored through the closer-to-physical bodies.

The Spiritual, Galactic, and Causal Bodies

If the mental body and Mind Grid are about thought forms and karma, the spiritual, galactic, and causal bodies are about creation. They are also about knowing and understanding who we are as part of Goddess/Source, as part of the Light, and about our place in creation as the result of our greater wholeness. Now that you have worked with the Lords of Karma and gone through the Essential Energy Balancing® process, you begin to understand what this means. The spiritual, galactic, and causal bodies are the place of the Higher Self, Essence Self, and Goddess Self, and the Goddess is beyond these levels. Also beyond the higher causal body is an ascension body that develops after completion of the Energy Balancing meditations. Beyond these still are many more levels and components of our Be-ing, more than we are now able to access or comprehend. Brede says that beyond the Goddess is Pure Light.

The spiritual body is the beginning of the Core Soul, and the lowest layer of energy that is not on a closer-to-physical level. Its outer octave is the causal body, which is actually two bodies, the lower and higher causal. The galactic body is the lower causal body, and the causal body itself is the higher level. This is not to be confused with the Causal Body chakra on the Hara Line, though the Causal Body chakra and Hara chakra are closer-to-physical access points for spiritual body energy. A highly developed chakra system exists on the spiritual body and is mirrored in the outer octaves of the galactic and causal bodies. I describe them as one system, but the chakras for both causal body levels exist in lesser form on the spiritual body octave below it.

The Celestial Template connects the mental body to the spiritual body. The I-AM Template connects the spiritual to the lower causal/galactic body and accesses the Higher Self. This is also where the Higher Self, Essence Self, and Goddess Self are brought from the causal levels into the spiritual body, and from there to the closer-to-physical bodies. Three Galactic Templates connect the galactic body to the causal body, and they also are the path the Essence Self takes to connect with the Higher Self. Three additional Causal Body Templates bring the Goddess Self/Oversoul in, to connect the Goddess Self with the Essence Self, and access connection with Goddess. Further templates beyond these access the Radiance of the Light beyond the Goddess.

Of the three Galactic Templates, the first and lowest operates through the Hara Line Thymus chakra in the Heart Complex. It is called the Intergalactic Template and offers contact with other planets and dimensions. We can communicate with the Ships through this template. The Ships are intergalactic other-dimensional transport that travel between worlds. Those of us living on Earth did not evolve here, we were brought here on the Ships, and some of us will go Home after ascension and this incarnation. Many people dream of the Ships, and some go to them during sleep for rest, teaching, and healing. During the time of healing my energy damage, I asked to be taken to the Ships for healing before I went to bed at night, and sometimes remember being there. The Ships are under the command of Ascended Master Ashtar and his women warriors, including the Goddess Athena. They are also protectors of our planet from other-dimensional negative interference.

The second Galactic Template connects in much-reduced form to the emotional body Hara chakra. Its purpose is in the ascension process, as the Energy Selves anchor into the closer-to-physical levels through this chakra. Our vibration must be much raised—through DNA reconnection, karmic release, and the clearing of negative interference—before this can happen. Our Energy Selves' vibrations must be reduced as well, as we could not hold their full energy without damage. It is fitting that this chakra which houses our life's work also houses our Energy Selves, the best of who we are. If your Goddess Self (or Goddess) chooses to anchor into you deeply enough for full manifesting on Earth, she will do so through the Perineum as well as through the Hara chakra. The third of the Galactic Templates is the place from which the Essence Self enters.

There are seven chakras on the galactic body and eight chakras on the causal body, plus the spiritual, galactic, and causal body Crown. All fifteen are mirrored in reduced form on the spiritual body level. The causal body chakras reflect the purposes of receiving spiritual information, usually by sound, and of creation that will ultimately reach earthplane under-standing or manifestation. The galactic chakras involve bringing this information from the higher causal body and beyond, into manifested Be-ing through the lower bodies. While receptivity is the keynote of the causal body chakras, the galactic chakras ex-press activity. These are opposites that do not conflict, but are two steps of a single process.

The chakras on the spiritual body, and the galactic and causal body outer octave, partly match chakra placements on the etheric, emotional, and mental bodies. They are located on the back, most of them along the spine. Again, these are higher level and outer octave chakra complexes, rather than the same chakras. They are not simply the back of the Kundalini or Hara Line, but are much-amplified energy that is closer to Source and to our real Be-ing. This is also true of the spiritual and causal body chakras that match those on the Hara Line and other chakra systems. The spiritual, galactic, and causal bodies share a single Crown chakra that operates through all three levels and connects them.

The causal body chakras are first, moving from the top of the body down. I have no color designations for these centers, and they are likely to be colors beyond the Earth body's visual spectrum. The chakras begin with a pair behind the ears that I have labeled *Sound chakras*. Many cultures attribute creation

DIAGRAM 19

The Spiritual Body Chakras

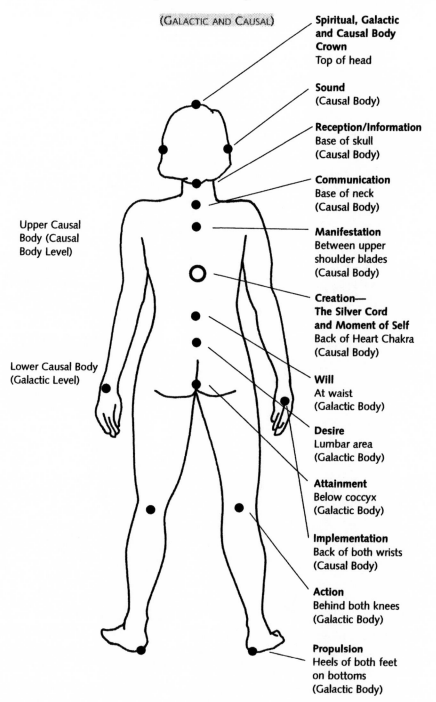

(GALACTIC AND CAUSAL)

**Spiritual, Galactic
and Causal Body
Crown**
Top of head

Sound
(Causal Body)

Reception/Information
Base of skull
(Causal Body)

Communication
Base of neck
(Causal Body)

Manifestation
Between upper
shoulder blades
(Causal Body)

**Creation—
The Silver Cord
and Moment of Self**
Back of Heart Chakra
(Causal Body)

Will
At waist
(Galactic Body)

Desire
Lumbar area
(Galactic Body)

Attainment
Below coccyx
(Galactic Body)

Implementation
Back of both wrists
(Causal Body)

Action
Behind both knees
(Galactic Body)

Propulsion
Heels of both feet
on bottoms
(Galactic Body)

Upper Causal
Body (Causal
Body Level)

Lower Causal Body
(Galactic Level)

DIAGRAM 20

Spiritual Body Chakra Energy Flows I

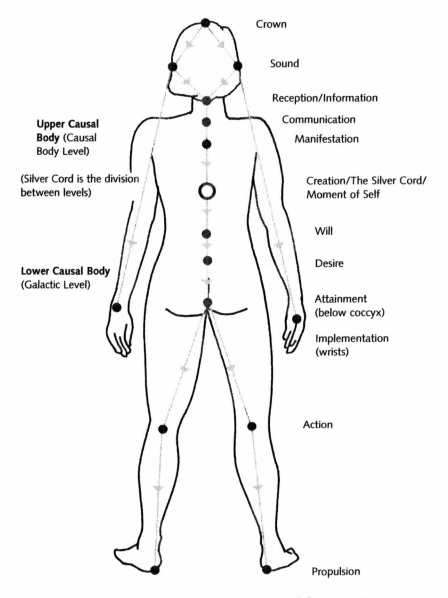

Crown

Sound

Reception/Information

Communication

Manifestation

Upper Causal Body (Causal Body Level)

(Silver Cord is the division between levels)

Creation/The Silver Cord/ Moment of Self

Will

Desire

Lower Causal Body (Galactic Level)

Attainment (below coccyx)

Implementation (wrists)

Action

Propulsion

Energy flows from Crown to Ground. Additional flows on Upper Causal Level move from Silver Cord to Crown, and flows on Lower Causal Level move from Silver Cord to Ground. All Flows are on the back of the body. Implementation chakras are on the Upper Causal Body Level.

DIAGRAM 21

Spiritual Body Chakra Energy Flows II

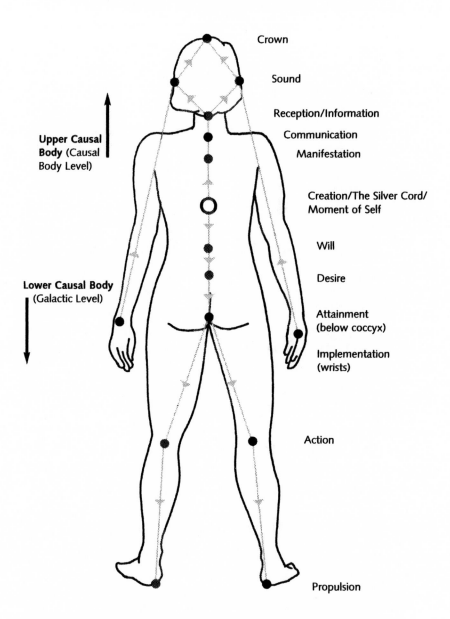

Crown

Sound

Reception/Information

Communication

Manifestation

Creation/The Silver Cord/
Moment of Self

Will

Desire

Attainment
(below coccyx)

Implementation
(wrists)

Action

Propulsion

**Upper Causal
Body** (Causal
Body Level)

Lower Causal Body
(Galactic Level)

Upper Causal Body Level—energy moves in either direction.
Lower Causal Body Level—energy moves downward (toward feet)
only. Implementation chakras are on the Upper Causal Body Level.

to sound, as in Buddhism's Om, the sound that created the universe. Some cultures define creation as both sound and Light, and Light is located beyond the causal body, as well as lower in the mental body system. Next is the *Reception/Information chakra*, located on the back of the head where the skull and neck meet. This is a higher octave of the Causal Body chakra on the Hara Line, where spiritual communication and channeling are received. The Causal Body chakra and Reception/Information chakra are different octaves of the same process, and both are part of the Throat Complex that contains the creation blueprint for all the bodies on all octaves and levels.

The third chakra of the higher causal body series is the *Communication chakra*, located at the lower Throat on the back of the neck. This chakra is for spiritual speech, and it takes the data of Sound and Reception/Information and expresses it. On the lower octave of the mental body, this chakra is the spoken union of body, mind, and spirit. The process so far takes universal sound/creation and translates the information into human sound/creation or spiritual speech. The *Manifestation chakra*, on the spine below the neck, continues this process of bringing creation from Goddess down through the levels. The chakra relays creation (Sound chakra) into existence (Manifestation chakra) by way of understanding (Reception/Information chakra) and expression Communication chakra).

Next in the process is the *Creation chakra*, located in the center of the back at the Heart, Heart Complex, and Silver Cord. Where sound is Goddess creation, this chakra is the human spiritual variety. It continues the process of translating energy from Goddess to Earth. The last in this series, the pair of chakras on the back of each wrist that I have named *Implementation chakras*, brings spirit into form through human work. All of these are receptive in nature.

The series continues and the process completes with the active Galactic chakras. Below the causal body Creation Chakra, at approximately the waist, is the *Will chakra*. This is a higher-octave chakra of the Solar Plexus Complex. *The World Book*

Dictionary defines will as "the power of the mind to decide and do; deliberate control over thought and action." This is in keeping with the Solar Plexus chakra, as the etheric lowest level of the mental body and Mind Grid. It is spiritual will, in this case, however, as energy from the causal level is always spiritual in nature. Will is another step in manifesting creation from Goddess to Earth.

Next is the *Desire chakra*. Desire is essential for action; before anything can happen or manifest, there must be the desire to bring it into Be-ing. Without desire there is no manifestation, as there is no impetus to bring idea (will) into form. As in the case of spiritual will, there is also spiritual desire.

Following Desire is the next galactic body chakra, that of *Attainment*. To attain something is to accomplish it. This chakra is located on the back below the coccyx (Root chakra), and is a part of the Root Chakra Complex. Creation at this point has come into Be-ing and form. Now it must reach Earth. To complete this, we are back to the knees and feet with a pair of chakras in each. On the back of each knee is a spiritual *Action chakra*, and on the heel of each foot a spiritual *Propulsion chakra*. These put creation and idea into motion, and the process begun with Goddess is finished on Earth. The spiritual/causal body chakras are a process for manifesting Spirit on Earth, bringing the information, manifestation, and grounding from Goddess to form. Though the process begins on spiritual and higher-octave levels, the energy transformers are chakra complexes that work through all the bodies. Because of this, creation reaches the physical, in however reduced a manner.

There are two energy flows for these chakras. In the first, energy (Light, Sound, Creation) moves from Crown to ground. Additional flows on the causal body move from the Creation chakra to the Crown, and the energy may move in both directions. On the Galactic body, however, energy moves only from the Creation chakra to the ground. These energy movement patterns are all on the back of the body.

The Silver Cord is a channel of Light that begins beyond the causal body level in the Heart Complex. It ends at the back of the Heart Chakra on the etheric body level. The Moment of Self also has its physical anchoring in the Heart chakra. The Silver Cord is our life connection. Its disconnection from the etheric body (physical/etheric level) signifies death and the end of the incarnation. During astral travel, some people see the Silver Cord trailing behind them as their Astral Twin flies.

The Energy Selves enter the closer-to-physical bodies by way of the Silver Cord and Heart Complex. After ascension is triggered, however, and the Energy Selves are anchored into the closer-to-physical levels, the Silver Cord withdraws back to the causal body level. This does not mean either death or the end of one's ability to astral travel. Instead, these functions are moved to the Crown. What it does mean, however, is that the creation process described in the higher and lower causal body chakras is now finished. With the merging of the Energy Selves, and anchoring into the Hara Line of one's Goddess Self (or Goddess), plus the connections with Goddess and the Light beyond Her, creation has been brought into form. The Goddess Self or Goddess has come to Earth. Her coming into form in physical bodies also raises the vibration of the physical, and so the process runs in both directions.

This information on Core Soul structure has been only rudimentary at best. We are as complicated in our energy as we are in our bodies, and the physiology of all the bones, organs, blood vessels, nerves, and processes in the dense body is an analogy of the complexity of our energy Be-ing. But physiology has been studied more, whereas we have lost the knowledge of who we are beyond the physical level. While the information is complicated, it is also fascinating. It is good to even begin to know who we are and what we consist of in our real selves.

Ascension

This final chapter is an attempt to explain what happens in our energy after ascension is triggered by Essential Energy Balancing®. As the meditations progress, you first meet and then anchor in the three Energy Selves—Higher Self, Essence Self, and Goddess Self—plus your connections with Goddess and the Light beyond the Goddess. Then the Energy Selves are merged into two sets. In one set, the Etheric Double and Astral Twin are fused, and the Higher Self is merged but not fused with them. In the other set, the Higher Self, Essence Self, and Goddess Self are merged and fused. Finally, the sets and Selves are all fused into one Be-ing, and that one is almost always your Goddess Self.

The rest of the Energy Balancing meditations are designed to raise your energy to a vibration high enough for the Goddess Self to enter and remain in your closer-to-physical levels. This primarily means clearing more than fifty percent of your Earth karma, reconnecting the DNA to twelve strands, and clearing and healing your Core Soul of all damage and negative interference. Once these are achieved and the fusion occurs, your Goddess Self is fully joined with you.

This is not the end, however, but only the beginning. As soon as the fusion of the Goddess Self completes and is sealed unto the Light and protection, in about three weeks, you are triggered into an entirely new process. This is the ascension process. In it, your energy vibration is raised to the fifth-dimensional level permanently, allowing your Goddess Self to remain permanently with you. It also clears more than fifty percent of your karma from your cellular levels (a deeper clearing than has occurred until this time), and finishes your requirement to reincarnate. While some people will chose to return to Earth to help others, and some are bodhisattvas doing this now, it will be a choice and not a requirement. When enough people have met this requirement and no longer need to reincarnate, the planet will be raised to the fifth-dimensional vibration as a whole, and karma will no longer exist here for anyone.

We are the beginning of a critical mass of ascended people, whose dimensional evolution will finally end karma. However, we are not the first wave of people ascending, but at least the second. There are descriptions in the New and Old Testaments of spiritually evolved people not dying, but being "taken up to heaven." Moses was granted this, as was Mary. Both may have learned the techniques for raising their vibration in the spiritual schools of Egypt. Moses was raised there, and Mary may have traveled there with Jesus when Jesus was a child. Scholars and psychics believe that Jesus did not die on the Cross, but instead returned to Egypt, or to India or Tibet, places that also had ascension information.

Buddhist teachings from these countries also describe the enlightenment of sages and teachers. In these stories, the great ones die, but within three days of death, their physical body disappears, leaving nothing behind but fingernails and hair. Tantric Buddhism talks about creating a rainbow body of light, evidence that at the moment of death the person has entered enlightenment. They define this as release from karma and from the requirement to reincarnate. Some metaphysical teachings describe enlightenment or ascension as being taken to a "pure land" or heaven where karma can be healed. These cultures usually place ascension at the moment of death, but this will not be the case in modern times. No one's body, alive or dead, will disappear.

We are entering ascension or enlightenment, but we are not leaving Earth. This is because Earth is entering enlightenment with us, and we are required to be here as the agents for it. It is not only a few people who will make their ascension in this lifetime (the enlightenment in this lifetime that Mahayana Buddhism promises), but the planet itself and eventually everyone on it. Animals are also increasing their vibrational levels to the fifth dimension; our pets may enter the ascension process with us. As Mahayana Buddhism states, we are not leaving anyone behind, we are all going together.

There will be other waves of ascension to follow ours, until everyone's energy is raised to the fifth-dimensional level. Eventually everyone will ascend, and everyone will be enlightened. Not only is the negativity, suffering, violence, negative interference, and karma being cleared from us, it is being cleared from the Earth and the Earth Grid, and eventually from everyone who lives here. Not only is our DNA being returned to the twelve-strand complement we were meant to have while being part of Earth incarnation, but everyone's DNA will finally be reconnected as well. The implications of this for a healed and evolved planet are tremendous.

For the individual, ascension means a multidimensional existence with complete conscious awareness of all the dimensions at once, and the ability to travel with awareness among them. It means breaking through to unlimited knowledge, the Light and Sound of creation on all the dimensions, and bringing that Light and Sound back to creation and manifestation on Earth. Ascension means expanded awareness and instant manifestation. It also means instant karma, with the healing of all potentially karmic events immediately, without suffering and without carrying them forward to other lifetimes.

Ascension is not as easy, however, as doing ten meditations and asking the Lords of Karma to fix everything. There is a price to pay in the six months of energy repatterning that follow. Though the process can be difficult, it eventually ends and it is worth going through it to experience what comes after. What follows the six months is everyday living with and as your Goddess Self. But first come the energy clearing, cellular repatterning, and changing energy structures. These are an initiation in the style of the ancient mystery schools, but where the ascension process in these schools took years to complete, it happens much more rapidly and more intensively now. This is because the Earth is in too much crisis to wait years for us to heal her. Because she needs us now, the process of healing ourselves has been speeded up. The following information will help you to understand what you are feeling and experiencing while the changes occur. It is based on my own process, and yours may be the same or different.

Early in the six months, you will experience seven to ten days of deep emotional pain. This is from the clearing of the karmic suffering carried in your cellular structures. During this time, your Crown and Transpersonal Point chakras will be kept closed. It is necessary for this to happen because each of your energy bodies will be taken off-line in turn for complete rewiring and repatterning. More than fifty percent of your Earth karma is being removed from your energy, not only from your Mind Grid and mental bodies, but from all the bodies down to the physical. This period will be longer and more difficult if you are bringing in a Goddess, instead of your Goddess Self.

Though ultimately very positive, all of this is quite uncomfortable. Closing the Crown causes you to temporarily lose all your psychic abilities. If you are a healer the energy will not come through your hands, and this can be quite frightening for those who depend upon it and who have always found it there. Your psychic hearing and vision will be shut down during this time as well, and you may also find your physical vision and hearing intermittently affected. There is physical discomfort in the tightening sensations of your Crown. With the Crown and Transpersonal Point closed, you will be mostly out of contact with your Goddess Self, Goddess, and the Lords of Karma, as well as with any other discarnate guidance that has always been there for you. This can be very upsetting, but understand that they have not left you when you need them the most. They are working on you and waiting nearby.

These chakra closings trigger every fear and emotion that your karma has programmed you with. If your overwhelming emotion in life has been fear, you will feel overwhelming fear. If it is anger, then anger will almost consume you. If you have been abused in any way, those emotions will come to the fore-front, and those who have been abused may experience a longer process until all of the abuse patterning is cleared. You may cry all night for several nights, feeling that you are alone and have been totally abandoned. It is important to remember that all of this chaos is the removal of old pain, and to understand it as pain leaving you forever.

The main part of this is over in about a week, but the emo-tions and Crown closing will recur intermittently for several months. During these times, there is nothing you can do but be gentle with yourself, and be aware that it will eventually end. You may wish to be alone for much of this period. Knowing what the process is makes it easier, and having faith in Goddess helps along the way. The worst is over once this is finished.

Along with cellular repatterning and the rewiring of all of your closer-to-physical bodies, a number of very interesting and exciting changes occur in your energy. You will develop another energy body, beyond the causal level, called an Ascension Body. This gives you access and communication with the Ascended Masters, the supervisory board beyond the Lords of Karma. You will probably meet Nada at some point, and some of the others, as they will become directly involved in your healing and ascension.

When you begin to see equations and formulas in your en-ergy, that seem to have no meaning, you are probably being worked on by St. Germaine. He appears in a purple robe and his violet flame transmutes all negativity and karma from your bod-ies. If someone asks you what's wrong and listens to your woes for hours, it is probably El Morya. Ask who is there and get to know them. You will learn a lot by watching them and asking what they are doing.

Someone from the Karmic Board will bring a series of col-ored ribbons and string them through your Crown and Causal Body chakras. You will feel them being pulled through, and these chakras may intermittently feel stuffed for a while. The first ribbons will come in pastel colors (mine were purple and blue), and the next set will be silver and gold. This happens about two months into the ascension process. These ribbons expand within your energy to make multidimensional travel in your physical body possible. Additional ribbons will be connected to your arms, legs, and wrists, and your arms and legs may feel sore, asleep, or peculiarly numb while this is happening. Your back may also hurt. The ribbons in the wrists bring in the full presence of your Goddess Self, and they are Ascension Body connections.

While this is happening, your Silver Cord is being withdrawn from one body at a time, from the causal body down. Since you will be traveling with the colored ribbons instead of astral traveling, and since your Energy Selves are already fused and no longer need a pathway, the Silver Cord is obsolete. Journeys out of the body now happen through the Crown. When you die, instead of disconnection, you will leave through the Crown and Crown Complex, taking your physical consciousness with you. This is what is meant by those who define ascension as not having to die. With multidimensional psychic travel through the Crown, instead of astral travel through the Silver Cord, you will not be disconnected from your closer-to-physical bodies at death, but will take them with you.

Another thing that occurs in the process, about three months into it, is the removal of information crystals that are no longer needed or positive. These crystals have been for karmic programming, Earth limitation, aging, living within time, and the requirement to reincarnate. None of these things apply to you anymore once ascension is complete, and the crystals are like used-up computer chips in your energy. They are like empty film cans, no longer relevant or useful after the film is developed.

Occasionally one of these crystals may seem stuck in your energy, and it feels like your Crown is being closed up again. Ask the Ascended Masters or the Lords of Karma to have the crystals released and removed, if you are told that it is time to do so. Their removal is a great relief, and you will begin to feel good about what is happening to you from here on. You will also begin to have contact again with your Goddess Self, if you haven't already.

At this point, you may ask the Lords of Karma for healing, reconnection, and activation of your twenty-one strand DNA. If they grant it, the reconnection will begin immediately, though it may take some time to complete. If they refuse it, ask if it can happen later. Those women bringing in a Goddess, instead of their Goddess Self, will be granted this, and probably some other women will be granted it as well. Our normal DNA complement while experiencing Earth incarnations and being part of this planet is twelve strands. The full complement, however, is thirty-eight strands.

The next, and one of the most major, changes in your energy is the removal of the family imprint. This will happen about three months into the process, soon after the other information crystals are gone. The family imprint is another information crystal, but it is a more complicated process to remove it, and removal may bring up more old emotions for a while. The family imprint is all those negative karmas, negative beliefs about who you are, and negative thought forms about life on Earth that are instilled in you by your family. If you have had a wonderful childhood, this release will be easier than for the majority of us who haven't. When I asked Nada what this removal would mean for me, she replied, "complete freedom at last." You may not realize how profound a healing this is until it is done. You may also find afterward that you no longer remember some of the abuse you received, or some of the terrible family situations.

Now you begin to bring your Goddess Self back and join her totally with your raised vibrational energy. Twice daily or more, and especially at bedtime, ask her to join fully with you by using the term "I-AM presence" in your request. She is your I-AM presence. The term seemed hokey to me until I tried it, but it brought Brede in closer than she had ever been before. Something in our energy systems are coded to this term, and it activates the joining. Use it repeatedly. As your Goddess Self merges into your energy, you will feel a tremendous sense of bliss that increases and remains.

As she fills each body, and fills all of the chakras on that body, you may ask her if she wishes to be tied into the chakras or to have the bodies sealed (unto the light). Tying into each chakra happens only once at each body level. If she says it is time, ask the Lords of Karma to tie your Goddess Self into each of the chakras on that body level. Work from the lowest chakra up, and ask for the tying into each chakra in turn. Your Goddess Self will ask you to seal the bodies frequently and repeatedly, and will do so each time she enters your energy to a deeper place.

It is important to frequently ask your Goddess Self (or Goddess) what she needs, and if there is anything she wishes you to ask of the Lords of Karma. She will tell you what to do, just keep asking and follow her instructions and requests. Each time that she feels fully connected with you is a good time to ask her what is needed. She may want the bodies sealed, or have you ask the Lords of Karma or a specific Ascended Master to increase her joining with you. The deeper she merges in, and the more fully she is joined, the stronger your sense of blissful wellness. This is where the difficulties of the process, which are now about over, become worth what it took to get past them. Ask your Goddess Self when you may request completion, and take that request to the Lords of Karma when she says it's time to do so.

Your Goddess Self is now living with you on Earth, and she may have some difficulties in adjusting. Earth is a chronically noisy place, and has sights and smells that are terrifying to an angel or a Goddess who hasn't lived in a body for some time, or maybe has never incarnated. Your Goddess Self will experience Earth through you and share your vision, hearing, and taste. You will enjoy her being there, but she may enter an initial time of culture shock. You will need to take care of her and help her. Ask her what she needs and how to do this.

When Brede first came in for me, sound was a particular problem. Her hearing is far more acute than mine is, and the urban electrical noises and other endemic background sounds were painful to her. Things I barely noticed, like the radio, refrigerator, air purifier, and air conditioner constantly running, discomforted her. The unpleasant high-pitched noises from an extended airplane trip and the noise of crowded airports were worse yet. Add to these a strong startle reaction to sudden loud noises and my Lady was quite often spooked and frightened. Though my life is a quiet one, I couldn't keep it as quiet as she needed it. After a offering her a pair of psychic earplugs and a psychic headphone did no good, I finally asked Nada to shield her from these overwhelming sounds. Nada helped, and it made a great difference for Brede's comfort.

Your Goddess Self may be frightened by the movement she sees through your windshield while you are driving, or made uncomfortable by sound as Brede was. Walking on a sidewalk next to traffic and crossing a busy intersection with a traffic light frightened Brede terribly. So did the temperature change of my entering a hot shower at first, or the first time she tasted ice cream. (She came to like the ice cream, however!) Your Goddess Self will taste what you taste, and see, feel, and hear what you do, but may not immediately understand what's happening. You, in turn, may experience heightened senses, or sometimes decreased senses, clumsiness, or spatial problems until you and she adjust to being together.

Along with these adjustments, your Goddess Self will also get into the spirit of the earthplane, and take joy and fascination with being here. I was delighted but not entirely surprised that Brede made my garden bloom extravagantly, that my dogs could see and play with her, or that her coming also brought a variety of small animals into the backyard. I was, however, highly surprised that she likes to go shopping, and that chocolate, ice cream, and popcorn are her favorite foods. She is not otherwise impressed with my cooking. Another friend who brought in a Goddess discovered that her Goddess likes to paint her toenails in extravagant bright colors. A different woman, bringing in her Goddess Self, tells me that her Lady likes black slinky dresses that she herself was never interested in wearing before. Yet another likes shopping for jewelry.

You may have more surprises, yet. I knew that Brede was a Maiden Goddess, but had no idea that she is fourteen years old fully grown. Then she decided that she wanted to grow up on Earth, so she came into me initially as a four year old and later at ten. Sometimes she appears fourteen to me, or adult, and other times as a small child. She took me to Toys 'R Us repeatedly one weekend and had me walk up and down every aisle several times. When I asked her what she was looking for, she said she was collecting ideas. She was interested in a rainbow-painted bicycle that said Mystical Passion on the side, but she didn't ask me to buy it.

She was also interested in, and did have me buy, several stuffed animals. When I thought about why she picked particular ones, it became clear that all of them looked real and all were endangered species. When I asked her about it, she said, "We're taking care of them." We have bought several more of these since. I occasionally get a psychic visual image of her sitting on my bedroom floor, a very small and delicate four year old, with toys strewn all around her. Occasionally she refuses to wear clothes, just to make me laugh, I think. She has sent other friends of mine shopping, too, appearing to them while they are in the stores. Once she wanted a box of chocolates, and on other occasions a small teddy bear, animal Christmas ornaments, a tote bag with giraffes on it, and a candle with seashells inside. No one can resist her, of course. Your Goddess Self or Goddess may surprise you in these or other ways; she may be a child or teenager, or any other age.

On another occasion Brede asked to go to K-Mart. I went, though there was nothing I needed there, and we walked around in the store. Finally, after going through toys and housewares, I asked her why we were there. She wanted "chocolates in boxes," and bagged candy would not do. We ended up with three pounds of boxed chocolate candy, and I asked her if she would take the calories if I ate it all for her. She decided that I could put them out for a Reiki class coming up. After the class, we were in another store and she found two more boxes on sale. She asks for some daily. She is a Goddess that likes chocolate and ice cream! By this time ascension begins to be a great deal of fun. You will be surprised at how deep your love is for your Goddess Self or Goddess.

Along with the Silver Cord being removed, other structural changes begin to happen in your energy as the ascension process nears completion. The first five templates merge into one, the I-AM Template. The Ka Template merges into the Etheric, both of which then merge into the Ketheric. The three then merge into the Celestial Template, and then the I-AM Template. Only one composite template remains, the I-AM, while the templates above it stay intact. Other mergings take place. All of the closer-to-physical energy bodies merge into one body, the spiritual body. The Mind Grid begins to disintegrate, too. Without karma, the information crystals, and the family imprint, there is no need for it to be there any longer.

The chakras also merge, and this is where the Heart Complex comes into it fullest opening. All the mental body chakras merge into one chakra, the Solar Plexus, first. Next, all the Hara Line chakras merge into the Thymus chakra, and finally, all the Kundalini chakras merge into the Heart. The Thymus and Heart are joined. Before merging at each level, the chakras' front-to-back openings are unsealed. Where the chakras formerly appeared cone-shaped on the front, with a much smaller cone on the back of the body, they now open fully into a tube that goes through the body from front to back. This happens on all three levels. You will feel spacey but well while this is occurring, and the opening will happen over a period of a couple of weeks.

Once the chakras are fully merged, the energy bodies merge also, and all the soul structure mechanics you have learned until now become obsolete. Nine energy levels and their chakras merge into three bodies and three chakras. Your new energy composition includes a first, second, and third body, as follows. The first body, which is soonest to form, consists of the causal, galactic, and spiritual bodies merged into one. The chakras from all of these merge into the Crown. The second body consists of the merging of the mental body and Mind Grid, with all of the chakras merging into the Solar Plexus. The third body is the last to form. It consists of the astral, emotional, etheric, and physical, and all of the chakras are merged into the joined Thymus and Heart.

As this is happening, your Goddess Self moves deeper into each composite level, and comes increasingly deeper into your consciousness and energy. Keep inviting her into your energy as your I-AM presence, and ask her (and the Lords of Karma) for her total merging in. Continue asking her what she needs and she will direct the process. You will see her, hear her, and feel her ever more deeply, and your feelings of wellness continue to increase. She will continue to be a separate Be-ing. While the bodies and chakras merge, continue doing the Process II Essential Energy Balancing® clearing. During the merging, you may add the request to "merge (the templates, bodies, and chakras) as appropriate" to the sequence of requests. After the full merging is finished, energy clearing is less often needed. If you have been doing it regularly, start asking your Goddess Self before you start it each time if it needs to be done.

While your Goddess Self will not come to you with karma or energy damage of her own to heal, if you bring in a Goddess, she might. Ask her if she needs healing, and what she needs. Ask her frequently, and you may be surprised at what she depends upon you to do. If she has damage or karma, you must heal her. To do this, you must go to the Lords of Karma for her. This is because karma can only be healed while in the body, and she is joined with yours. Once your Goddess comes in, she picks up any unresolved karma she may have had from any incarnation on Earth. Even if she has only incarnated twice into body on this planet, and the last incarnation was a thousand years ago, she may still have damage and karma to heal. This will be so for many of the Goddesses.

Your job in this is to ask her what she needs, and then to make the request as exactly as possible to the Lords of Karma. Take it through all the steps of karmic release. The Ascended Masters of the Karmic Board will be involved in this, but you will need to do the asking and to go through the process for her. Brede had serious energy damage to heal, a broken Galactic Cord that lost her connection and joining with me on a number of traumatic occasions until it was finally repaired. Because of this damage, she could not incarnate into body as she had wished to do. With the damage healed, she is savoring Earth life, chocolate, and shopping with me. Your Goddess may need healing, too. Ask her frequently, at least several times a day, if she is okay and if she needs anything, and if she needs you to go to the Lords of Karma for her or for yourself. If you do this, you will effect her healing and she will also direct and implement yours.

The last structural change in the ascension process is the completion of the Ascension Body and Belt of Light. As this ring of energy develops, it will surround your newly merged energy bodies, with you and your Goddess Self or Goddess inside. The purpose of this body is total energy protection for you and for your Goddess Self. It also offers permanent access to the Ascended Masters you have come to know since the ascension process first began. When you leave Earth permanently at the time of your death, you will be a member of the Ascended Masters yourself. You will hold the full presence of your Goddess Self within you for the rest of this lifetime, and join with her even more fully after it. Death will be only a change of venue, one more bit of multidimensional travel, and you will take your physical consciousness with you.

In the meantime you will not age, and your physical body will heal. You will be free of all the suffering you came into body with, and free of most of your karma with no new karma to accrue. You will be released from the negativity of the planet's mass consciousness, from all cultural and family negativity, and from all the negativity that has been programmed into your mind and Mind Grid. You will live long, and death will be meaningless because you are a multidimensional being. You already know what is on the other side and that there is nothing there to fear. At the end of this lifetime, you may be going Home to your planet of origin, or to some other bodhisattva assignment, but you will no longer be held to Earth by your karma. If you choose to come back here, it will be only by choice.

The ascension process is quite miraculous and worth the effort of the difficult months of clearing. You have been through an initiation and have prevailed, and are much greater in your Be-ing for having done it. Accept the great joy and many Goddess blessings that come from here on. You've earned it.

BOOKS BY THE CROSSING PRESS

Other books by Diane Stein

A Woman's I Ching
ISBN 0-89594-857-5
7 x 9 • 256pp • Paper

All Women Are Healers
ISBN 0-89594-409-X
6 x 9 • 292pp • Paper

All Women Are Psychics
ISBN 0-89594-979-2
6 x 9 • 360pp • Paper

Casting the Circle
ISBN 0-89594-411-1
6 x 9 • 260pp • Paper

Essential Energy Balancing II
ISBN 1-58091-154-4
6 x 9 • 176pp • Paper

Essential Reiki
ISBN 0-89594-736-6
81/2 x 10 • 158pp • Paper • b/w illus.

Essential Reiki Workshop
ISBN 0-89594-930-X
(ISBN 1-58091-016-5 PAL version)
4 video cassettes
Under 5 hours running time
A One Spirit Book-of-the-Month Club selection.

**Healing with Flower
and Gemstone Essences**
ISBN 0-89594-856-7
6 x 8 • 176pp • Paper

**Healing with Gemstones
& Crystals**
ISBN 0-89594-831-1
6 x 8 • 160pp • Paper

The Holistic Puppy
ISBN 0-89594-946-6
7 x 9 • 160pp • Paper

**The Lords of Karma
and Energy Balancing**
A Workshop with Diane Stein
ISBN 0-89594-977-6
(ISBN 1-58091-017-3 PAL version)
1 video cassette
1 hour, 20 minutes running time

Natural Healing for Dogs & Cats
ISBN 0-89594-614-9
81/2 x 10 • 190pp • Paper

**Natural Remedy Book
for Dogs & Cats**
ISBN 0-89594-686-6
6 x 9 • 341pp • Paper

Natural Remedy Book for Women
ISBN 0-89594-525-8
6 x 9 • 348pp • Paper

Prophetic Visions of the Future
ISBN 1-58091-046-7
6 x 9 • 240pp • Paper

**Psychic Healing with Spirit
Guides and Angels**
ISBN 0-89594-807-9
6 x 9 • 256pp • Paper • b/w illus.

We are the Angels
ISBN 0-89594-878-8
6 x 8 • 160pp • Paper

BOOKS BY THE CROSSING PRESS

Other books by The Crossing Press

Ariadne's Thread: A Workbook of Goddess Magic
By Shekinah Mountainwater

One of the finest books on women's spirituality available.—Sagewoman

Shekhinah Mountainwater's organized and well-written book encourages women to find their own spiritual path. This is a very good, practical book...recommended.—Library Journal

Paper • ISBN 0-89594-475-8

A Wisewoman's Guide to Spells, Rituals and Goddess Lore
By Elizabeth Brooke

A remarkable compendium of magical lore, psychic skills and women's mysteries.

Paper • ISBN 0-89594-779-X

Chakras and Their Archetypes: Uniting Energy Awareness and Spiritual Growth
By Ambika Wauters

Linking classic archetypes to the seven chakras in the human energy system can reveal unconscious ways of behaving. Wauters helps us understand where our energy is blocked, which attitudes or emotional issues are responsible, and how to then transcend our limitations.

Paper • ISBN 0-89594-891-5

Mother Wit: A Guide to Healing and Psychic Development
By Diane Mariechild

It is a joy to find this material from occult traditions and Eastern religions adapted by her woman-identified consciousness to the needs of women today.—Womanspirit

Paper • ISBN 0-89594-358-1

Spinning Spells, Weaving Wonders: Modern Magic for Everyday Life
By Patricia Telesco

This essential book of over 300 spells tells how to work with simple, easy-to-find components and focus creative energy to meet daily challenges with awareness, confidence, and humor.

Paper • ISBN 0-89594-803-6

For a current catalog of books from The Crossing Press,
visit our web site: **www.crossingpress.com**